CHICKEN SOUP FOR THE SCRAPBOOKER'S SOUL

CHICKEN SOUP
FOR THE
SCRAPBOOKER'S
SOUL

Stories to Remember . . .

Jack Canfield
Mark Victor Hansen
Allison Connors
Debbie Haas

Health Communications, Inc.
Deerfield Beach, Florida

www.hcibooks.com
www.chickensoup.com

We would like to acknowledge the following publishers and individuals for permission to reprint the following material. (Note: The stories that were written by Jack Canfield, Mark Victor Hansen, Allison Connors or Debbie Haas are not included in this listing.)

An Egg-Splosive Hobby. Reprinted by permission of Ginger McSwain. ©2004 Ginger McSwain.

Out of My Way! Reprinted by permission of Nancy Ann Liedel. ©2005 Nancy Ann Liedel.

When a Hobby Is More Than a Hobby. Reprinted by permission of Stacey Wakelin. ©2005 Stacey Wakelin.

Confessions of a Scrapbooker's Husband. Reprinted by permission of Joel Doherty. ©2005 Joel Doherty.

(Continued on page 289)

Library of Congress Cataloging-in-Publication Data
is available from the Library of Congress

©2006 Jack Canfield and Mark Victor Hansen
ISBN 0-7573-0409-5

Publisher: Health Communications, Inc.
3201 S.W. 15th Street
Deerfield Beach, FL 33442–8190

R-07-06

Cover and inside graphics ©Doris Castle
Cover design created by Andrea Perrine Brower
Inside book design by Lawna Patterson Oldfield

With love we dedicate this book
to all of the scrapbookers who share our passion,
addiction and devotion to this wonderful craft.

We also dedicate this book
to our family members—Tom, Heather,
Mary Kate, Tommy, Steve, Jason and Adam—
who are our inspiration. Without all of you,
we would not have the wonderful
memories of life to treasure and
remember forever and ever.
We love you all!

Contents

3. CONNECTED TO THE PAST

4. FROM THE HEART

5. OVERCOMING OBSTACLES

6. A SCRAPPER'S PERSPECTIVE

Acknowledgments

We wish to express our heartfelt gratitude to the following people who helped make this book possible:

Our families, who have been chicken soup for our souls!

Jack's family—Inga, Travis, Riley, Christopher, Oran and Kyle—for all their love and support.

Mark's family—Patty, Elisabeth and Melanie—for once again sharing and lovingly supporting us in creating this book.

Allison's family—to my wonderful husband and best friend, Tom. You have been there through thick and thin, supporting me with your love and encouragement. Even when you thought my decisions lacked better judgment, you still allowed me the freedom to follow my dreams. You are my soul mate, my love and my life. To my oldest daughter Heather, I marvel at the woman you have become—from a little peanut looking up at me to a beautiful friend who shares many of my passions in life. You are truly an inspiration to me and a tremendously bright light in my ever-growing world. To Mary Kate, your irresistible sweetness mixed with your quirkiness always keeps me on my toes. You are an exhilarating young girl, an astonishing delight and a hidden comic, and I love spending time with you. You are the flower that blossoms anew every day.

To Tommy, your kindness and thoughtfulness are immeasurable. You amaze me all of the time as I watch you reach out a hand to help others. You enjoy life to its fullest and have taught me not to be afraid of trying new things. You are my rock—dependable, uplifting, encouraging and always steady. To my loving mother, Audrey Norris Clancy, whom I have always looked up to—everything I am today is because of you. Your love, guidance and constant support have given me the tools to be a better person, a better mother, a better wife and a better friend. To my dear friend Patricia Nelson, whose steady support, encouragement and "idea bouncing" have helped me to be where I am in the scrapbooking world today—your friendship has been a constant in my everyday life. And last but not least, to my dear friend Debbie Haas—this book would not have been possible without you. Your sparkling personality and love of life are apparent with everything you touch. To all of you (and others I may have missed—you know who you are), I thank you from the bottom of my heart and love you all so very much!

Debbie's family—to my mother and dearest of all friends, Vera Laike Sebastian, who has guided me from the very beginning and taught me to be a wife, mother, daughter, fairy godmother and good friend . . . especially since I have always walked to the beat of my own drum, and sometimes the music of life was very loud! To my sweet and precious husband, Steve, you have always been the wind beneath my wings—thank you for always telling me to reach for the stars and for being my best friend. To Jason, my oldest son, you are the reason I started to scrapbook, so I could always remember all of the incredible pieces of life we have shared and will share. To my adorable Adam, who loves to scrapbook just like Mommy, you have so many special gifts, and you teach me every day what it is to love unconditionally. To all the amazing women in our Diva Chapter and "our good ol' friends in the hood," thank you for being there when I needed you. With Steve's deployment this year, you helped keep me on track. But most of all, I would like to say thank you, Allison Connors, for our friendship and your work ethics—I love you!

Our thanks also to:

Our publisher, Peter Vegso, for his vision and commitment to bringing *Chicken Soup for the Soul* to the world.

Patty Aubery and Russ Kalmaski, for being there on every step of the journey, with love, laughter and endless creativity.

Barbara LoMonaco, for nourishing us with truly wonderful stories and cartoons.

D'ette Corona and Noelle Champange, for being there to answer any questions along the way.

Patty Hansen, for her thorough and competent handling of the legal and licensing aspects of the *Chicken Soup for the Soul* books. You are magnificent at the challenge!

Laurie Hartman, for being a precious guardian of the *Chicken Soup* brand.

Veronica Romero, Teresa Esparza, Robin Yerian, Jesse Ianniello, Lauren Edelstein, Patti Clement, Maegan Romanello, Cassidy Guyer, Noelle Champagne, Jody Emme, Debbie Lefever, Michelle Adams, Dee Dee Romanello, Shanna Vieyra and Gina Romanello, who support Jack's and Mark's businesses with skill and love.

Michele Matrisciani, Andrea Gold, Allison Janse, and Kathy Grant, our editors at Health Communications, Inc., for their devotion to excellence.

Terry Burke, Lori Golden, Kelly Maragni, Sean Geary, Patricia McConnell, Ariana Daner, Kim Weiss, Paola

Fernandez-Rana—the sales, marketing and PR departments at Health Communications, Inc.—for doing such an incredible job supporting our books.

Tom Sand, Claude Choquette and Luc Jutras, who manage year after year to get our books translated into thirty-six languages around the world.

The art department at Health Communications, Inc., for their talent, creativity and unrelenting patience in producing book covers and inside designs that capture the essence of *Chicken Soup*: Larissa Hise Henoch, Lawna Patterson Oldfield, Andrea Perrine Brower, Anthony Clausi, Kevin Stawieray and Dawn Von Strolley Grove.

All the *Chicken Soup for the Soul* coauthors, who make it such a joy to be part of this *Chicken Soup* family.

Our glorious panel of readers who helped us make the final selections and made invaluable suggestions on how to improve the book: Katie Klink, Vera Klink, Vera Sebastian, Suzie Kigler, Bonnie Bartley, Corrine Mihlek-Bryzs, Teresa Clinton, Deanna Doyle, Patricia Nelson, Sherry Adaire, Terri Davenport, Lisa Helm, Mindy Ohoritey, Tonya Paul, Linda Sterling, Christie Snow, Joyce Simmons, Tracy Soares and Nancy Tackett.

To the wonderful people and companies who helped us to promote and solicit stories to make this book great—you all have been an invaluable tool toward our success: Jlyne and Noel Hanback of Scrap Submit (*www.scrapsubmit.com*), Two Peas in a Bucket, Inc. (*www.twopeasinabucket.com*), Danielle Forsgren—The Scrapbook Diva (*www.divacraftlounge.com*), Carol and Barry Tarling of Cruise Holidays of Barrie (*www.cruiseholidaysofbarrie.com*), *Scrapbooking.com Magazine* (*www.scrapbooking.com*) and Denise Pearlman of Scrapbook Attic and More in Arkansas.

And, most of all, thank you to everyone who submitted

their heartfelt stories, poems, quotes and cartoons for possible inclusion in this book. While we were not able to use everything you sent, we know that each word came from a magical place flourishing within your soul.

Because of the size of this project, we may have left out the names of some people who contributed along the way. If so, we are sorry, but please know that we really do appreciate you very much.

We are truly grateful and love you all!

Introduction

I t is said that a picture is worth a thousand words, but who puts those words to the photograph? The scrapbooker is the person who breathes life into photos, capturing the essence of the memory once created and now captured on film. The scrapbooker brings back the warm feelings, the exciting moments, the tearful reunions and the fond thoughts of moments past through journaling, careful selection of papers and intricate placement of embellishments. Scrapbookers are the storytellers of their lives and of those lives that have touched theirs in some special way—whether from generations past or generations to come. Scrapbookers put their hearts and souls into every page they create, no matter what the outcome may be.

This book is full of stories from scrapbookers just like you. They are heartfelt, funny, poignant, remarkable, happy and amazing stories written deep down from others to touch your soul and tickle your emotions. We all have a story to tell . . . whether it makes us feel like we belong, helps us through a difficult time or gives us bellyaches from laughter. Our hope is that you will be influenced and inspired by the anecdotes framed within each and every chapter, that you will be moved to tell your stories on your pages and to feel at one within the scrapbooking community. We are a sisterhood/brotherhood of scrappers; let's leave our mark on the world!

1

The Scrapbook Addict

It is not in doing what you like,
but in liking what you do that
is the secret of happiness.

Sir James M. Barrie

An Egg-Splosive Hobby

*Did you ever stop to think
and forget to start again?*

Winnie the Pooh

I really should be too embarrassed to admit this . . . let alone record it on a scrapbook page. But on the other hand, it just seems fitting to create a layout that only proves the point of the layout itself!

It began one early December afternoon. I decided to make egg salad for Kent for his lunch. I fed little Sam, and while he was eating . . . I put the eggs in a pot, covered them with water and turned on the stove. When Sam was finished with his lunch, as per our normal routine, I took him upstairs for his nap. As I left his room, I felt an undeniable pull to my scrap area in the upstairs playroom. It was like a giant magnet pulling me in, and once I got my hands on all those photos, cardstock and my favorite trinkets and gadgets . . . well, think kid in a candy store! All reason (not to mention memory) flew out the window.

Oh, I scrapped happily . . . just a few stolen minutes. I'd get to the laundry in a while. The minutes piled up. They became over an hour.

I remained in my adhesive-coated blissful state until the sound of a sudden and loud popping jarred me to my senses. What was THAT? For a moment I feared Sam had fallen out of bed. I raced to his room. He was sleeping peacefully. Hmm, what could that have been? Oh, well . . . very willingly I dismissed it as the "pull" returned and took hold of my consciousness again. I returned to my scrapping. There it was again! This time I began to wonder WHO was throwing rocks at our house!? POP! . . . and again I heard it. As I approached the top step of the stairs, I suddenly had a frightening realization . . . THE EGGS!!!!!!!

In almost a single step, I landed at the bottom of the stairs and raced to the kitchen. At first I was terrified as I confronted a black-bottomed, smoking pot with eggs that were bursting one at a time . . . well, more like blowing up. I quickly turned off the stove, shoved the pot off the heat and stood back to survey the damage. My kitchen was covered with exploded eggs.

After the shock, not to mention the horror at the realization of what COULD have happened, I began to clean up the mess. After finishing the cleaning of the floor, I began to see the humor, and like any scrapbooker worth her glue, I grabbed the camera. Lesson learned. Now when I feel the magnetic pull of all those photos and that yummy cardstock, I ALWAYS go to the kitchen first to check the appliances.

Ginger McSwain

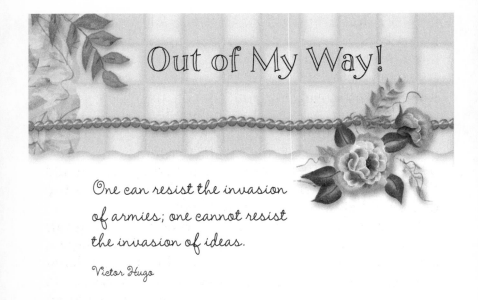

Out of My Way!

One can resist the invasion of armies; one cannot resist the invasion of ideas.

Victor Hugo

"OUT OF MY WAY! I have an idea. Move it!"

Off they go scattering like dry leaves on a breezy fall day—four kids, a dog, a cat and a husband who know those words mean business. Mom is scrapbooking, and inspiration has struck! Well, to be honest, inspiration may come at any moment over anything, usually in the shower, which is why I have been known to scrap in a towel. Abandon the computer, don't get near the scrap-space, "everyone out," she is "at it again!"

Okay, so I am half nuts—my family would say "more than half"—but when inspiration smacks me in the nose, getting out of the way is the best, and safest, idea. Not moving fast enough has been known to cause frustration and grief. There was the time my toddler did not get away from me with all due haste, and I took a pair of scissors to get a lock of his hair. It would have been okay if he hadn't moved. I suppose the bald spot can be combed over till it grows back.

My seven-year-old knows that when I have the camera in hand, he had better be on his best behavior or his worst will be caught on film, notated and scrapped. I am certain future generations will want to know all about his fart jokes, really. My poor infant can't crawl yet, so he is made the subject of all sorts of odd layouts. All I can say for him is that perhaps he should thank his lucky stars that I have not been motivated to do a layout about a diaper change yet.

My husband has learned that nothing is sacred in this house when it comes to his "obsessed wife." Duct tape, a screen door repair kit, hinges he bought to fix the bathroom door, even playing cards have all been sacrificed to the scrapbook demon living inside me (who I have named "Mo"). My poor husband doesn't even ask anymore when some implement is missing from his toolbox; he just heads to my scrap spot—which is very well organized, I swear. Just because no one else can figure out where anything is does not mean I am not the Queen of Organization.

Anything and everything is fair game when I am on a scrapbooking tear. There is not a store I have been to that has not had items placed on my pages. From the grocery store . . . a scan of a bag containing coffee for an "Addiction Page." From the hardware store . . . easy, practically every aisle is represented. (One of these days, I am going to do a layout with a carpet remnant. I just need the right "spin.") From the animal feed store . . . well, in pages about our pets, of course. The rare store that does not have actual product in my books is represented by photographs; after all, what is a book in relation to our lives without pages regarding an average day?

Fonts are another "problem area" of mine. When complaints started registering in my beleaguered husband's brain about the slowness of my computer, a quick peek (okay, okay, it took three minutes for the file to open, it was so large) into my font folder illuminated the problem. I am not sure why four thousand fonts would slow things down so badly. I think Microsoft Word should be able to handle all those, don't you? I am now limited to one thousand active fonts at a time. Dire warnings about consequences having to do with my ability to journal and print were levied in my general direction from my techie husband, who was trying to look stern. He was so adorable I grabbed the camera and took several photos to scrap later. I can see the title now: "Why You Should Not Have 4,000 Fonts" or "Font-O-Holics Anonymous."

By the way, limiting fonts is completely unfair! How can I find the perfect look for my journaling with such a small selection to choose from? Perhaps I should start a letter-writing campaign.

Time seems to be another issue. Because we have four small children, I am often too busy with them during the week to scrapbook, which means I play "catch up" on the weekends. Translated, that means I go into long scrap sessions that you cannot pull me out of even with the promise of fresh-brewed coffee and Krispy Kremes. I suspect if the house was on fire, I would not notice till some hunky firefighter dragged me out, and even then I would have to take notes for scrapbooking later—it is not every day you are saved by a hunky firefighter. Often I look down at ten A.M. only to look up again at five P.M. wondering where the time went. Since I am the chief cook and bottle washer around these parts, I still have to make dinner. Rachael Ray and her "30-Minute Meals" have nothing on me. I can prepare a five-course dinner in fifteen minutes, and that includes the time it takes to open the cans and start the microwave!

Why is this so important to me? Why do I get excited on days I plan to attack the local scrap store? Despite the many references to a "midlife crisis" by close friends and family (who all get scrap projects for birthdays and Christmas), it is more than that. Scrapbooking allows me a creative outlet. It gives this forty-one-year-old mother of four, two of whom are in diapers, time to grow and learn something precious about herself. It offers me a break from "Mommy, he is looking at me" and "The Wiggles." Scrapbooking inspires me to reach beyond who I am expected to be and attain something that is simple, special and sacred—creation itself.

Nancy Ann Liedel

Reprinted by permission of Mack Dobbie ©2005.

When a Hobby Is More Than a Hobby

Dare to dream—don't be afraid to aim for the highest peak . . . it is there we see all that is possible . . . all there is to hope for—dare to dream.

Author Unknown

When does a hobby become more than just a hobby? Perhaps when it becomes a part of you and not just an activity to pass the time? When it fulfills your dreams? Well, I guess scrapbooking is more than just a hobby to me. I remember the day I was introduced to the craft of scrapbooking. At the beginning, it was merely a new craft to try—playing with papers and scissors. I also remember the day I became hooked. It was after my first son Evan was born. A beautiful little baby had entered our lives, and all of a sudden scrapbooking developed new meaning. I wasn't just gluing papers together; I was creating a book filled with Evan's childhood memories.

I quickly became devoted to recording every milestone in my albums. It was also at this time that I came to realize the impact this craft had on my life. It renewed my passion for creating, something I had put on the shelf since childhood. This hobby was now a part of "me." I would stay up until the wee hours poring over my scrapbook layouts. My layouts were no longer just for my young son; they were for me—a part of me that I was convinced would never blossom, the part related to artistic endeavors and dreams. I had always loved creating, whether it was a delicate dessert or a short story. However, I had convinced myself these were just silly childhood fantasies. I would never create a masterpiece or see my creations in a gallery or magazine. But wait, all of a sudden here I was creating works of art. True, they were not created on canvas, but works of art nonetheless. I was using paper, bits of metal, ribbon and—most important—my life to create these layouts.

My heart went into each layout. Each layout became more personal; I had taken the photos and written the words on each page. I was becoming acquainted with a whole new world. My love of scrapbooking gave me the key to this alternate universe. I pored over magazines filled with new products, ideas and passion for this craft. Suddenly, everything I had believed about myself and my dreams had changed. Fellow scrapbookers were being published every day. These artists were not famous, but ordinary housewives and mothers just like me.

It was at the exact moment that I gave myself the permission to try, that my life changed. I decided I was good enough to be published in a magazine and decided to start submitting. I did so and doubted myself for months. Then one day, I received an e-mail that fulfilled my desire. One of my projects was going to be published in a scrapbooking magazine. It was with shock, disbelief and pride that I shared the news with my family. Suddenly, nothing seemed impossible. All I had to do was believe in myself and put myself out there. The rest would be taken care of. Soon more e-mails poured in from the magazine; they would like to publish more of my work.

Filled with a new confidence, I decided I had other dreams I wanted to see fulfilled. Along the way, I felt a sense of guilt. Here I was spending time pursuing these goals when I should have been simply satisfied with the life that I had. I had immense blessings that already filled my day: a happy marriage, a loving family and the ability to stay home and care for my son. Why should I need more? I ultimately decided that the time I spent on scrapbooking was time reserved for me. The part of the evening after the kids were put to bed, I spent creating and renewing myself. Once I gave myself permission to continue, the road ahead seemed filled with opportunity. The creative world that was so large and far away suddenly became smaller.

I truly believe once you open yourself up to the possibilities, you open yourself to success. Now, almost six years after dabbling with the hobby of scrapbooking, I consider it a part of who I am. I am most certainly a wife, mother, daughter and sister first, but deep down I am also an artist. I find myself amazed at how scrapbooking has enriched my life. I am part of a large, worldwide community that speaks a special language. I am privileged to teach new scrapbookers and share my excitement with them. These classes and gatherings have created friendships and bonds that didn't exist before. I am lucky enough to have fulfilled many dreams through this hobby.

I think I just answered my own question. When does a hobby become more than just a hobby? The answer is: when it transforms the dreams and ambitions of a person, when it becomes more of an adjective than a verb. I don't just scrapbook, I AM a scrapbook artist. For someone who always dreamed of having the arts become a part of her life, that is a big deal!

Stacey Wakelin

Confessions of a Scrapbooker's Husband

From the glow of enthusiasm I let the melody escape. I pursue it. Breathless I catch up with it. It flies again; it disappears; it plunges into a chaos of diverse emotions. I catch it again; I seize it; I embrace it with delight.

Ludwig Von Beethoven

I pulled my truck onto our gravel drive after a long day's work, with the anticipation of being greeted by my lovely bride and our three children—clean, well mannered and ready for bed, awake only because they had begged to stay up long enough to say good night to Daddy. It was a pleasant, wholesome image and made me smile as I grappled with my truck for my briefcase. Successfully freeing the case from the cluttered interior, I made my way to the front door.

All the lights were on, and as I opened the door I was greeted by my two-year-old, who was decidedly not ready for bed, but was, in fact, wrapped rather impressively in embellishments. I bent down and looked at him closely. Yes, that was some Creek Bank Creations Twill E Dee twill tape wrapped around his chest, and a woven label that said "All Yours" was stuck on his forehead. Various other pieces of ribbon, cloth and fibers completed his predicament. This was probably the work of my four-year-old daughter, but it might also be my wife's handiwork, particularly if our son was being meddlesome, which he generally was.

"What's doing, Luke?" I asked.

He paused from licking the filling out of a tiny s'mores cracker, carefully placed the licked cracker halves back in the box and smiled at me. I thought I detected a few photo tabs stuck in his hair.

"Where's Mom?" I asked.

"Scrappin' 'oom," he said, returning to his crackers.

Ah, scrapping room . . . of course. I needn't have asked.

"You want me to untangle you?" I asked before I went to the scrapping room, which used to be our bedroom but was now really a products warehouse with a bed in it.

"No. Wan Anna Madada," he said after some thought. Hakuna Matata, words from *The Lion King*. "Okay, but only for a minute." I fired up the DVD for him and headed down the hall to the scrapping room.

I rounded the corner to our room and paused in the doorway. There was product everywhere. My wife is extremely talented, but she tends to be one of those people who take their creativity from the chaos around them. Our computer, which my wife insisted I upgrade repeatedly to handle her design criteria and is now so powerful that

NASA leased it to search for unknown star clusters when my wife isn't working on it, was humming away. Two printers were merrily spitting out pages. The whole setup reminded me of those Bloom County cartoons where Burke Breathed would draw the computer two feet off the desk, bouncing madly around while it worked.

The room had two eight-foot folding tables set up on a fairly permanent basis, and our four-year-old was sitting on one of them amid heaps of my wife's discarded pictures and embellishments. Beka, our daughter, also scraps, rather well actually, and she uses just about anything she finds, but particularly items my wife doesn't need from whatever layout she was currently working on. She was cutting out something with deckle-edged scissors, and her little brow was furrowed in deep concentration. My wife was sitting at the same table, studying a type gauge sheet over a layout.

"Hi, Honey, I'm home."

She turned around, an excited smile on her face. Hmm. This was good.

"Guess what!" she demanded happily.

"What?"

"I won the Regional Pseudo-County Scraptopia Contest!" Or something like that. Uh-oh. Now was the critical moment. My wife entered a lot of contests, and I didn't even try to keep them straight. However, for the health of my marriage and my own happiness, I always tried to appear to keep them all straight. I thought quickly. I knew she had mentioned this awhile back. That was the problem with these things—sometimes the results were three or four

months down the road. I couldn't remember my own
stuff for three or four months. The dentist had to continually remind me where his office was for my six-month visits, even though he hadn't changed offices and I'd been
his patient for fifteen years.

She'd said something about a ten-thousand-dollar contest. I tried to gauge the look on her face. That was
another problem. She tended to get excited easily where
scrapbooking was concerned, and it was hard to judge
the magnitude of the event from her own reaction. It
didn't look like ten grand worth of excitement, though.
Crap. I couldn't remember any other contests. I was running out of time. I had to say something, something
appropriate, and fast.

"Wow, Honey! That's great! The Regional Scrappseudo-
topia . . . Wow! That's great!"

She started telling me about the contest. Whew. This
must be a pretty big one. She was so excited she didn't
notice I was dancing like Fred Astaire.

". . . and do you know what I get for winning?"

More product. "What?" I exclaimed.

"An all-expenses-paid getaway for two to San Diego!"

Holy smokes! That was really something. Good gosh,
maybe there was something to this whole scrapbooking
thing after all. All those contests and this was a big one,
and she'd won. This could really be the start of something.
A getaway! Wow! We'd have to beg my parents to handle
the kids, but I'm sure they could do it . . . two nights or just
one? Who cares, this'll be great. I was starting to get
excited about scrapbooking.

"Isn't it great? A scrapbooking weekend. I'll take
Shannon, and they've set it up so we can scrap the whole
weekend with all this cool stuff!"

The party music playing in my head came to a screeching halt with the sound of a record needle being dragged across the vinyl. Scrapbooking weekend? Oh, well. I embraced my love and gave her a big hug. "Congratulations, Honey, that's really wonderful. I'll watch the kids; just tell me when."

The really crazy thing was that I couldn't help getting caught up in her enthusiasm. I glanced around at all the tags, labels, ribbons, photos, eyelets, rivets, stencils, stamps, papers, inks, paints, pastels, cutters (a technical term), squeezers (another technical term) and couldn't help but think it might be fun. Of course, I was the guy who wrapped my wife's Christmas present by setting it in the middle of the wrapping paper, gathering all the ends together and wrapping them tight with duct tape—sort of the pineapple approach. But still.

"So, Honey," I said, putting my arm around her as we walked out to get the kids ready for bed, "are there any guys at these things?"

"Yeah," she said, looking up at me. "Some. Why? You interested?"

"Maybe," I allowed. "But I'd need something. Maybe if I could wear my John Deere hat, then it might be okay."

She laughed. The dog went by with a Paper Bliss fish stuck in his tail. Yeah, I could really get into this. I started making plans to get the bed out of the scrapbooking room. Who really had time to sleep, anyway? Right?

Joel Doherty

Only Five Dollars

There are more important things than money—the only trouble is they all cost money.

Louis A. Safian

As I near the store, my heart begins to race. Thoughts of gloriously colored, patterned paper, textured cardstock and exciting new embellishments enter my head.

"No!" I say. "Only five dollars. I can spend only five dollars today. I already have so much at home. I need only a few things." I slowly take a deep breath and get out of the car.

I'm walking through the door. I forget how much I love this place—my special place where everyone understands my need to put photos on paper, add embellishments until my pages buckle, and they certainly understand my need to purchase new items. I grab a basket, grasping it tightly in my fist, hoping some of my excitement will seep into the handle and out of my body so that I can stick to my goal. "Only five dollars."

As I turn, I stumble into the "New" section. "No!" I say. "I need only a few things." But wait a minute, I've never seen that sticker before. "Oh, and surely I don't have any paper in that color and pattern." I look and touch and handle. Suddenly, my arm feels heavy. I look down to see my basket near to overflowing. "How did that happen?" I ask. Surely I didn't put that much inside the basket. So I stop at a nearby table and review my items. "Oh, I suppose I can do without those letter stickers. And I can wait until next time to get that paper." I whittle down my items until my basket is much lighter.

"I should probably check out," I think. "Well, while I'm here, I'd better make sure there isn't anything I need." So I walk the aisles reaching out to touch each item. It feels like a dream. So many things, it all begins to look the same. I walk the aisles one more time. I add only a few more things. In this calmer pace, a bit of guilt begins to creep inside my conscience.

"I had better check out," I sigh. I wait in line and refuse to look at my basket. Secretly I know I've missed my goal. "Only five dollars," I remember. "Well, certainly that wasn't reasonable. Surely I will need these things," I tell myself.

Then it's my turn, and the cashier is ringing up my items. I avert my eyes from the register and thumb through the idea books at the counter. I'm cool, calm and collected. "I'll just pretend like I meant to spend this much," I decide. Then the cashier gives me the total.

"Fifty dollars," she says.

"Fifty dollars!" Halfway through a gasp, I recover. "Fifty dollars," I say, trying not to shake as I hand over my credit card. While she's running the card, I'm doing math in my head, moving around figures, trying to think where I will

find fifty dollars. "Well, I won't drive so much this month. We won't eat out so much. I can return that new shirt I bought." Trying so hard to justify my purchases, I hardly realize that I'm signing my name on the receipt.

In a daze I leave the store. *"Fifty dollars! Fifty dollars!"* I think. Repeating the total doesn't make me feel any better. I'm halfway home when I realize I forgot to get the adhesives I needed.

Jennifer S. Gallacher

The Scrapbook Store

I went to the scrapbooking store today
Just to buy one thing,
Then I saw this layout on the wall
It made the products sing.

Oh, I need to have those stickers
Showcased on the rack,
I've only got two things in my basket
No need to put one back.

Wait, now I see those flowers
Oh, maybe just one or two,
My shopping has turned into
Buying not one, but a few.

Look, there's some pretty paper
With polka dots galore,
I need it for my layout
I've got to have some more!

Brads, eyelets and ribbons
My collection is getting low,
Just add these to my shopping spree
It's almost time to go.

Now, I found some albums
You never have enough,
Leaving this store with just one thing
I'm finding very tough.

Okay, that's it, I'm done now
I bring my stuff to pay,
I look at my watch to see the time
Have I been shopping here all day?

Allison Connors

Coming Together

Many hands make light work.

Greek Saying

My mother is a scrapbook junkie. Not your normal, "I-scrap-every-day" junkie. This woman is obsessed. The large upstairs room (the scrapbooking room) hasn't had a visit from a vacuum cleaner in years; going in there without a hard hat and a pair of hiking boots is hazardous to one's health. But this isn't enough. The dining-room table mysteriously reappears for family gatherings and then returns to the abyss until needed again. The living room couch is so well covered, it is not in any danger of ever fading, and the two card tables that reside in our family room are strictly off-limits to anyone else. That also applies to our kitchen counter. There is no place to set anything where a scrapbook supply will not be in danger.

My mother's bedroom is littered with ziploc bags that she uses to store scraps of paper in, and her desk is covered with scrapbook magazines, planned swaps, expo information and more fonts for her journaling than a publishing company would have use for. I, on the other hand, can easily contain all my scrapbook supplies in one box.

That's all I need. But stay home while my mother goes shopping for scrapbook stuff? Perish the thought! You see, most scrapbook supplies are sold in stores that also sell sewing supplies. At this point, I should probably point out that I am an avid cross-stitcher. My mother scraps, I stitch, and the evenings pass quietly between us.

One day, however, my mother wasn't scrapping, and I wasn't sewing. Oddly enough, we were both  reading. This is a hobby we share. I saw my mother search for a bookmark and finally use an index card when I had a glorious thought. I got out a prefabricated stitchable bookmark. I put yellow roses on it, my mother's favorite flower. I labored for three months before it was completed. I then presented it to my mother so she could mark her books with something better than an old index card. She could maybe put it in her Bible. It was so pretty, and I handed it to her with a flourish. She was very pleased; she hugged and kissed me and told me it was a lovely surprise and a lovely bookmark. It was her next remark that started me sewing more avidly than ever. She smiled and said, "I'll use it in my scrapbook." It just so happens that my mother, who sewed a good deal before her eyes went bad, wanted some pretty cross-stitched things in her album, but couldn't see well enough to do it. Now, when she sees something that she wants in her album, she hands it to me, and I sew it and return it. Maybe my mother is a scrapbook junkie. Maybe I'm a sewing junkie. And maybe, just maybe, that's what makes us close.

Alonnya Schemer

The Morning After

This morning I wake up and open my eyes just a little bit, tiny slits. Light pours in . . . SHOCK. I feel something; what is it? Small hands are poking at me. I hear something; is it talking?

A sweet little voice says, "Mommy, can you get up?"

Get up? Me? Why? I think to myself in my state of sleepiness.

I hear the patter of more little feet. And then I hear another sweet voice saying, "Mama, mama, mama."

Then she comes into view, cute little grin, then, "Oh, hi." Now that I'm more awake, I realize that I am in my own bedroom. And these beautiful little creatures buzzing about me are my children. Still a little groggy, I'm not sure why my whole body feels so heavy or why I'm so very tired still. My husband walks in and says it's time for him to get to work. As the entire family thumps down the stairs to the kitchen, there are little voices, one yelling, "I'm the line leader," the other saying, "Baba, please . . . please."

In my state of grogginess, I walk past my dining room, and there it is on the table . . . the evidence. I faintly recollect last night . . . my girlfriends were here. I am remembering the glow of all the lights, the happy chatter, the laughter and our conversations, one running into another. It comes back to me clearer now—talk of our families, our children, our childhoods, our dreams, our goals, our lives, our jobs, our friends, our homes, our trips—all of us conversing into the wee hours of the morning.

On my table, among the plates, cups, napkins, scraps of paper, magazines and books, lies my completed project for the evening. I stop to admire my work—the colors work, the layout works and the embellishments are great! As I think about the events pictured in my layout, I feel enveloped by my dearest friends. I remember the warm and happy feelings around the table the night before. Not only have I created something meaningful for my family to look back on, but each page of my scrapbook is a reminder of the wonderful friendships I have cultivated through this hobby and a memory in itself of our time together.

It's all so worth it to be a little fuzzy before my coffee this morning.

Just then, my reverie is broken by a chorus of little voices—"Mommy, what's for breakfast?"

I smile lovingly at the little ones, give hugs and kisses all around, and as I make them breakfast, I think to myself, *Time to start our day . . . time to make another memory.*

Marnie L. Bushmole

Rest and Relax on a Three-Day Retreat

What fun you will have on a three-day retreat,
Cutting and pasting with short breaks to eat.
The friends you will see; the ones you'll find;
Everyone comes to get away from the grind!
You're crazed from being deprived of slumber;
You pound out the pages, increasing your numbers.
The pain in your back is hard to mistake;
Ignore it—keep going—you're creating keepsakes.
Then it's your eyes, the dark circles and bags;
Never mind that, I made five new tags!
You sit and eat, someone's constantly cooking;
Burning off the calories with aerobic scrapbooking.
Then pack it all up, say good-bye to your friends;
Sadly enough it has come to an end.
Even more sadly—and you know it's so—
You were wearing the same clothes, three days ago.

Paula Gunter-Best

When White Lies Turn Dark

You don't have to fool all of the people all of the time—just the right people some of the time.

Millard's Conclusion

Many times, scrapbookers simply need to minimize the recognizable purchases made for supplies and materials. It's not that we are ashamed; this is just an addiction for which we desire no cure or treatment. Besides, a lot of our purchases are for basic supplies—they are necessities, right?

My web of white lies turning dark began quite innocently. I had the pleasure of winning a contest sponsored by an online retailer. The prize was a package of scrapbook materials valued at more than twenty-five dollars. I was elated at my good fortune and proudly proclaimed this to my partner. When my prize package came, I quickly sorted through my winnings and again reveled in the delight of my victory. The next week I had the honor of serving on this same site as the guest designer of the month. Again, I received a prize package filled with incredible goodies. Once again, I proudly displayed my accomplishments. At the end of the month, once again, I won a monthly layout contest through my local scrapbook store; hence a gift certificate to the store. The stage of deceit was set.

Several weeks passed, then a package arrived for an order I had placed online. Mark called to let me know the package had arrived. I cringed. We had just discussed budgeting and had each agreed to reduce the amount of expenditures on our respective hobbies. I agreed to reduce, but not eliminate! But I knew the arrival of this package would meet with skepticism and disapproval. It was not a lot of money, and they were things that I needed. My stomach filled with knots as I prepared to explain my order.

My fears quickly subsided, as did the knots in my stomach, as Mark told me, "It must be another prize package; you are so lucky." I agreed and proudly accepted his congratulations for my accomplishment, although I did feel a little guilty. This was too easy! From that point on, every order that arrived at my home became a "prize package." After all, it was not out of the realm of possibility. It had happened, and it could happen again, right? I had entered a lot of contests, so I could conceivably win a lot of prizes. Several months passed. I scrapped happily and ordered new materials as they were released.

But invariably white lies turned dark . . . when I had the opportunity to meet one of Mark's business colleagues. As I was introduced to her, Mark told me she was also a scrapbooker, so we already had something in common. We chatted for a few moments and discussed the possibility of getting together to crop one afternoon when she

replied, "I don't know; I am not nearly as good as
you are. Mark has been telling me how many contests you have won!" Modestly, I accepted her compliments, replying, "Well, I have won a couple."

She was stunned. "A couple! Mark says you get a prize
package delivered at least every other week!"

At first I thought Mark had just been making a big deal
out of the two contests I had won—until I arrived home.
There on my porch was the latest "prize package" from my
favorite online retailer!

Paula Gunter-Best

"I'd like to thank the academy and all the little people who made this possible."

2

A Sisterhood/ Brotherhood

It is at times such as this that we show our true spirit of giving and of brotherhood—of revealing the "Good Samaritan" in all of us.

Jo Bonner

More Than a Message Board

One's life has value so long as one attributes value to the life of others, by means of love, friendship, indignation and compassion.

Simone de Beauvoir

On October 4, 2002, at 2:30 P.M. a seventeen-year-old boy, following the lead of a forty-two-year-old man, fired a bullet that forever changed the life of a scrapbooker in Fredericksburg, Virginia. While loading her van in the parking lot at Michael's craft store, she was shot in the back by the "Beltway Sniper," who terrorized the Washington, D.C., area for the month of October. While she was "lucky" in that she survived her encounter with the snipers while ten people did not, she will carry the scars forever.

I lived in Fredericksburg when this happened. I shopped at that Michael's on a regular basis. I did not, however, know this woman. All I knew was that I was horrified, frightened and outraged that this horror was unfolding in my own backyard. I felt helpless and frustrated, and turned to the one place I knew I could pour out my feelings and receive the comfort and support I so desperately needed— the Creating Keepsakes Message Board. I had been a very active member of this scrapbooking message board for several years.

As I told the story and vented my feelings, the other message board members were, as always, more than kind and concerned. They shared my frustration that there seemed to be nothing we could do that would have any effect on this terrible tragedy playing out in my area. However, as brains got churning and ideas began to brew, a plan did emerge. No, we could not change what had happened or what was to come, but perhaps we could make a small difference by sharing our sisterhood with this woman whose life had so suddenly and violently been turned upside down.

The packages and cards began pouring in from all over the world—not just from Americans, but from people in New Zealand, Australia, Canada and Germany. They came from everywhere to make a gift basket for this person we did not know by name, but felt a kinship with by heart. By the time another scrapper from the message board and I delivered the basket, it was huge, overflowing with prayers, cards and good wishes—and enough scrapbook supplies to provide countless hours of diversion during recovery. It was a basket filled with love. Later, another basket and book would come, as gifts trickled in over the months, the message was clear: We are a sisterhood, bound by a common thread and hobby, but more than that, no matter our race, religion or nationality, we are children of the same God, born with the same loving, giving hearts, sharing the same fears and the same joys. We are an awesome group, this sisterhood of ours, and I, for one, will be forever grateful for being a part of it.

Kathy Freeman

With a Little Help from My Scrapbooking Friends

Friendships multiply joys and divide griefs.

Thomas Fuller

At seven months pregnant, I liked to start the day slowly with a leisurely breakfast. I took my time getting ready to start the day, waking up with a little music on the radio. Although I bounced about the house humming "Mambo Number Five," I had a nagging feeling that something was wrong. Was it the baby?

I went about my day, heading to the grocery store. On the drive home, I heard a sad song on the radio. There was that feeling again—something was wrong. With autumn approaching, I was in the mood for comfort food and began preparations for a Sunday meal. As I methodically chopped carrots, celery and potatoes, the feeling remained. A sinking, sad feeling grew when the phone rang. I heard my husband talking and knew it was not good news. My brother called to inform us that something had happened to my father. We immediately drove to the family farm, not expecting the news we were about to receive.

As we pulled in, I saw unfamiliar cars lining the farm driveway. My heart raced as I ran inside the kitchen. Normally the gathering place for family holidays, the farm kitchen was always filled with scents of baking and cooking. Today it was filled with the faces of policemen and other official personnel. *Where is my father?* I wondered. By the looks on their faces, I knew it was heartbreaking news. The rest of that day is a horrific blur as I learned the details of my father's tragic death.

Traumatized by the distressing news and very pregnant, I had to be checked by my OB-GYN. My husband and I were reassured to hear the steady heartbeat of the baby. My doctor told me everything was fine and gave me some medication to calm my nerves. I was able to get through that awful week, planning the arrangements for the funeral and doing my best to support my grieving mother.

During the funeral, several people approached the family. My father's coworkers, people we had never met before, thought very highly of him. Apparently, he helped many of them through difficult times of their own. Learning this information was both comforting and inspiring. After the funeral, we gathered for more tears and sadness. Drained and tired, I wanted to be home in bed, but the day would be long. Although friends and family tried their best to console me, there was no comfort that day.

My baby arrived three weeks early, healthy and beautiful. I couldn't help but see my father's face in my newborn son. My life was about to change dramatically. I was no longer a library director, my father had died, and I was now a new mother. I don't think the full impact of my father's death hit me until soon after the baby's birth. Sleep deprived, I was faced with being alone day after day without my job to distract me.

Depression set in quickly. I felt isolated and alone, having a baby in the winter months, staying inside all day. One of my hobbies before the baby was born was scrapbooking. I found it difficult, however, to work on preserving cheerful memories while such sadness permeated my life. Instead, checking my e-mail became my favorite task of the day. In the deep cold of winter, it connected me to the outside world, and I could do it with the baby on my lap, in the comfort of my home.

It wasn't until I found a group of online scrapbooking friends that life began to change. I started visiting online message boards and joined a group through Yahoo. I discovered a whole new world of friendship and fun. I joined swaps with several friends and eventually decided to host one of my own. Some of the girls in my very first swap have become my closest friends—from the East Coast to the West.

The heavy weight of my father's death began to lift. I became more involved in my hobby, eventually joining a design team and having layouts published in magazines and online. I am now able to work from home, spend time with my children and enjoy every minute of my amazing life. Through scrapbooking, I am reminded each day of life's blessings. Today I am fortunate enough to work for an online magazine and design for several scrapbooking companies. In the days following my father's death, I would never have thought such an incredible life was possible.

Life is never easy, and as soon as you conquer one challenge, another presents itself. When my son was four years old, I learned he has Asperger's disorder, a mild form of autism. With the support of my scrapbooking friends, I discovered others in my group with special-needs children. We e-mailed almost daily about our challenging children, sharing both parenting advice and layout ideas.

Scrapbooking brings people together, whether it's at a monthly crop group or an online message group. They are caring, thoughtful people who share supplies and are eager to help friends learn this wonderful hobby. They love to look at each other's scrapbooking creations, sharing stories and memories, whether they are happy or sad.

I have met some of my best friends online already, and hope someday I will meet the rest. With much gratitude, I thank this group of women for helping me through a difficult time. I only hope I can do the same for them should they need me someday.

Deanna Doyle

Unexpected Friendship

s a teacher of middle-school children, scrapbooking has become a way to capture my students' interest in writing beyond the standard five-paragraph essay. Not only does it stimulate their writing skills, but it also awakens the artist within each child.

Because scrapbooking supplies are not included in our school budget, I have always requested donations from manufacturers and store owners. Most companies are receptive to my inquiries. Of the many e-mails I send out for these requests, one day I e-mailed a woman named Carrie at her online store. She replied immediately with an enthusiastic response toward my scrapbooking program. When she sent the supplies, I was amazed by her extreme generosity. She sent enough products for each of my students to create pages for the entire year! I felt that a simple e-mail thank-you was not enough, so I called her.

We spoke on the phone with the ease of old friends, even though I had never met her before. We talked that day about my students, her daughters, my sons and her online scrap-booking community, which she encouraged me to join. I registered that afternoon, and quickly Carrie and I began to foster a friendship unlike any other I have had in all my life.

In the last year, our friendship has grown to depths that continue to amaze me. Recently, she told me that she feels a connection to me. When I am sad, she knows. When I have a migraine, her head hurts. She is the first to call me when she thinks that I am upset about something. She listens when I cry. She laughs when I tell her my typical "Colleen got lost driving" stories. She defends me when she believes I am not being treated fairly. She inspires me constantly. I tell her that she is my mentor. She is that and so much more to me.

When Carrie and I met, it was at a point in my life when I had recently struggled with health issues that left me scared. When I am stressed, my typical reaction is to retreat within myself, not letting anybody close. At that particular time, I was so far locked into my fears that I was miserable . . . and lonely. Carrie saw that in me and, gently, she brought me back. She taught me to release my fears through my art. I became an artist because of her.

Sure, I had already been scrapbooking for years, but Carrie taught me that art has no boundaries. She forced me to see that I could write my thoughts, my fears and my feelings directly on my scrapbook page. That was when I started my *Book of Me*. Through my friendship with Carrie, I began to heal.

In my search for supplies, I wasn't looking for a friend, but I found one—it was certainly an unexpected friend-ship. And for that, I am truly blessed.

Colleen Stearns

Sometimes It's More Than Scrapbooking

I had a splitting headache from studying my company's budget all afternoon, and things were not looking good. My landlord had called earlier in the day to tell me my son and I were out if I missed one more rent payment. So I was counting the minutes until I could go home and get into a hot bath, maybe one of my last, when Doloros Shanton fell into my scrapbook store. Yes, she literally fell, as her medications had caused a brief dizzy spell and she tripped over the doorjamb. I ran to her side, helped her up and sat her in the nearest chair. After half a glass of water, she apologized for the drama she had caused and explained that she was not well. She had recently been diagnosed with colon cancer and was currently undergoing some physically exhausting treatments.

As we spoke, she told me about her desire to preserve her life in some way now that she knew it was ending. She was hoping to put as many memories as possible into scrapbooks to leave as a legacy for her future generations. I was overtaken with sadness for this frail, old woman who was now facing her last hour. I promised to help her in any way that I could.

Doloros came to my store every day after that, and we began to build her legacy. She was in her eighties, and I was quite sure we would not be able to finish before the cancer would overtake her. Some days we would work together creating the pages. Other days, she was so drained that she could only watch me and offer suggestions. After a while, she became so weak that we moved our efforts to her home, and I went there daily to help complete this awesome task we had started. It became a driving force within me. My mountains of problems seemed so miniscule when compared to this noble effort of a dying woman. I had not felt such passion in many years. I had come alive due to a dying woman's last request.

Doloros's medical condition remained quite consistent throughout our time together. It was only in the end, when we had completely documented her life in the books, that she felt it was time to let go. I sensed it from her, as if her work on Earth was complete. I still continued to visit Doloros; we had become wonderful friends. We talked about her life, and it felt like I had known her forever.

During one of our last conversations, Doloros told me there was still something unsettled in her mind. She said that she had lived in her house for many years. It was very dear to her, and she feared what her family would do with it once she was gone. She told me she had been looking for someone she trusted to be the next owner, and she asked if my son and I would live there for her.

At first, I couldn't speak. I just began to cry. Although I had never mentioned my financial situation to Doloros, things had been steadily getting worse during the time I had known her. My son and I had never owned a home, and I was truly overwhelmed. She hugged me and told me that nothing would make her happier than to have us live in the place she loved for so many years.

After Doloros passed, my son and I moved into her home. We felt as if her arms were outstretched to us as we walked through the door for the first time. We have lived here now for five years, and it is as if she never left. Sometimes I sit and recall the short time I spent with Doloros Shanton, and I remember her telling me that I was an answer to her prayers. It always makes me smile because I know that, many times over, she was an answer to mine.

Holly Pittroff

Friends Forever

My friends have made the story of my life.

Helen Keller

Several years ago I attended a sorority convention in Indiana. I became fast friends with my suitemate, Jill. We went to all of our sessions together and had so much fun. We cried when we left each other at the airport and vowed to stay in touch and try to see each other again. We stayed in touch for about two years, mostly through Christmas cards and typical correspondence. Then I got married, moved away and we lost touch with each other. I always remembered Jill and kept her picture with my others. I wondered what happened to her and what she was doing, but I didn't think I would ever see her again.

Last year over my Christmas break, I was visiting a popular scrapbooking Web site that I frequent. I responded to a message asking for anyone in my area who would like to get together and scrap. Since I hadn't lived in this area for too long, I didn't have many friends who were interested in scrapbooking like I was. I was excited to meet someone who lived nearby and would share my love of scrapping. As I began to e-mail back and forth with the person on the other end of the computer, a lot of things began to sound familiar. In the last e-mail before things became clear, the woman said she had to go back to Ohio to pack up her house because they had sold it recently. Her name sounded so familiar to me, I just had to ask. "Are you an ADPi?" I asked her in my e-mail. I explained how her name and information sounded so familiar to me. She e-mailed back, "Are you Sarah Jacobs?" Of course, that was my maiden name, and she was my long-lost friend Jill. Unbelievably, she had moved from Ohio to about thirty minutes from me. We began to e-mail back and forth right away and talked to each other that weekend.

From then on, we have rekindled our special friendship. We scrap together and have shared many of our lives' moments together . . . all because of a scrapbooking Web site.

Sarah Higgins

Scrapbook Boy

A boy's best friend is his mother.

Joseph Stefano

My son, Devon, had just turned twelve. As I watched him blow out the candles on his cake, I got nervous. I wondered how my son's universe would expand and how I would fit into it.

My son was so different from me. He loved science; I loved music. He adored computers; I couldn't tell a byte from a modem. He enjoyed rock music, while I favored Mozart.

I knew we needed to do things together to keep close, but it wasn't easy. He grumbled while we hiked the Rockies, as I gushed about the spectacular views. He delighted in camping. I hated the mosquitoes.

Then one day, by accident, we found an activity we could share. I was sprawled on the floor, working on scrapbooks. Devon asked if he could make a page.

I admit, I was surprised. I didn't think my son would get excited about paper hearts and cutesy borders. I showed him a few basics, expecting him to lose interest after a few minutes.

Imagine my surprise when he didn't. He analyzed color combinations with the scientific scrutiny that was his trademark and went wild with photo captions (loving the gross ones I ignored). It wasn't long before he'd completed a page about an autumn camping trip, remembering the yellow aspens and the smoky smell of the campfire.

He proudly showed me his finished page. He was heavy-handed on the stickers, but for a first effort it looked great. I expected him to head outside, but he didn't. He made another page.

We laughed as we sorted snapshots of Devon as a bald baby and an obstinate toddler in red overalls. By the time we were finished, we'd both completed several pages. More important, we had remembered how much we share.

Devon is now sixteen. Like most teens, he's absorbed in the whirl of high school. Although he now relegates the cutting and pasting to me, we still like our scrapbook time.

We smile as we look through photos of past Christmases. He offers opinions about layouts for pictures from his trip to Paris. We sit on the couch and look through his albums, remembering and laughing, forgetting that we are different, my son and me.

I don't tell him I think tearfully about future pages of his high-school graduation and first college dorm room. I still have pages to make of his next birthday and senior prom. And time to share them together.

Lisa Ray Turner

The Scrapbook Lady Taught Me Love

Deeds of kindness are equal in weight to all the commandments.

The Talmud

t was finally happening! A scrapbook store finally opening in my town. Before this, the closest store was one hundred miles away. That was finally about to change. I watched eagerly as the shelves filled with papers, stickers, eyelets and all the other delights that only a scrapbooker can appreciate. My nose would press against the glass like a child window-shopping at Christmas. It was magical. My only worry was my son. A lot of stores don't like children, but I quickly learned this was not a problem.

The owner called out, "Hey, little man, why don't you come and talk to me?" She amused my five-year-old while I quickly browsed the shelves I had dreamed about.

Over the next few months, Jared frequently asked to visit the Scrapbook Lady, and she told us to come back often.

"Don't worry about buying anything in my store—just come and visit with me often," she'd tell us.

Sometimes we'd walk by her store when it was closed. If Jared saw the Scrapbook Lady, he would wave, and she would open her door to get her hug and daily news. She pulled me aside one day and told me how special she thought my little man was. She made me promise to bring him back soon, but next time we went, she wasn't there.

Our hearts sank as we learned we wouldn't see her again. She had found out that very week she had cancer in her brain and lungs, and it was spreading throughout her body. She wrote a good-bye letter to all of her customers, saying that she would be closing her store. The next day the women rallied and filled her store. Some were there to shop; some were there to help. The Scrapbook Lady's daughter struggled to keep up with the crowds.

I have always told my friends that I love my hobby because I meet the most wonderful people. I know that to be true because as the clerk labored to keep up with the line, someone stepped up and started putting all of the purchases in a bag for her. As I looked around, women were fixing the shelves, filling in any open spots and organizing merchandise. Our friend needed help, and those of us who loved her pitched in.

The store exuded a feeling of love that spread throughout town. Anywhere I traveled within our city, someone was talking about the Scrapbook Lady and how she was coping with her illness.

I was standing on line at the mall, not meaning to eavesdrop, when I heard the news. A woman talking on her cell phone mentioned "scrapbook," and before she finished her sentence, I blurted out, "The Scrapbook Lady died?" My heart sank. It took me a moment to realize that I wasn't the only voice crying out. The woman on the phone looked shocked that we all knew who she was talking about, but told us of the Scrapbook Lady's passing. She went on to say that her final days were filled with grandbabies, scrapbooking and going to church. This woman looked confused that we knew who she was speaking of, but she didn't realize we were scrapbookers; we were the Scrapbook Lady's friends.

The Scrapbook Lady made everyone feel like they were the most important person in the world. She sold the perfect paper and accents to make a page perfect; she gave us the heart of scrapbooking for free. We scrapbook because we love others, and we don't want our memories forgotten. She loved us all, and for a woman who didn't lead a famous life, she will not be forgotten. She lives on in our hearts and in the pages of a little man's scrapbook.

Heather Ellis

Circle

If you love someone, put their name in a circle, not a heart, because a heart can be broken, but a circle goes on forever.

Brian Littrell

We were just random members of an online scrap-booking message board—and we were all very brave to open ourselves up to each other, total strangers. We were drawn together by our love of this craft and another common bond—probably the most painful thing that has ever happened to us. I believe that we were all a bit surprised at how difficult it was to discuss the loss of our children. I know for me, it was unbelievably painful when I got right down to it. But I was excited, as well, to try this idea of a circle journal that one of the ladies suggested. I think we all were.

I gathered my supplies and began making a memorial to my daughter Molly, a stillborn twin. She had died of unknown causes in 1998, and I had wondered how I would overcome my grief. She was special. How excited we all were for her to come join our family! But as so often happens, that was not meant to be. So, wiping my tears, I created a book of love for her.

As I prepared to send it around the country and even the world, where people would add to it, I said a little prayer that somehow Molly's story would touch others, that in her own way, she would make a difference. I sent it off, from my hands to another's, uncertain about this journey and where it would lead me.

Then I got the first journal, Tara's, and I remember crying in a most heartbroken way. Reading her words, I wondered how I was going to get through this. But I did. I wrote from the heart about my precious Molly and how she died, how her departure left a hole in my heart, how we as a family moved on, never forgetting, but moving on as time would have us move. I mailed Tara's journal off to Trish and breathed a sigh of relief. I had done it!

Then Amber's journal arrived, bringing with it a new level of sorrow and grief. How shocking her loss was . . . how much I could feel her pain. My oldest son was diagnosed with a brain tumor at two and a half and has battled it ever since, ten long years. Surgery successfully removed part of it when he was five, but the remainder is there, pressing against his brain stem like a time bomb. I could relate to her story. Grief-stricken for her loss, I cried some more and then moved forward, remembering my sweet baby, sharing my memories of her for Amber, hoping that in our grief, she would find comfort and strength in numbers . . . hoping that all of us would.

Each month another journal arrived, filled with stories of love and loss, heartbreak and hope. Each month, I cried; each month, I shared; each month, I grew. With each journal I completed and sent on its way, I grew stronger.

Our circle is not yet complete, but I look forward to the day when Molly's journal returns to me, and I can hold it in my hands and feel the love conveyed on its pages. I hope in the end that I can use my circle journal for good. I teach scrapbooking classes and offer a "Scrapbook Pages That Heal" class. This is something I hope to share in those classes. I also work with our local Pregnancy Loss Support Group—what a wonderful opportunity to share with those families ways to hold on to the memories of their little ones.

A circle is a never-ending shape, like the love we have for our children. Living with the loss of a child has been and will be a journey. But each step I make forward is a step toward tomorrow and what it holds. I am glad for the journey.

Cynthia Chan

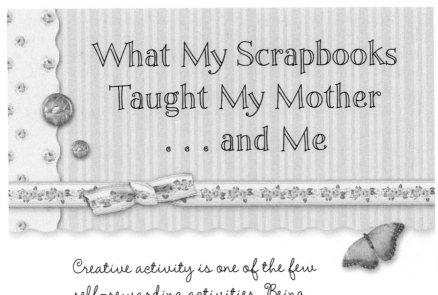

What My Scrapbooks Taught My Mother ... and Me

Creative activity is one of the few self-rewarding activities. Being creative is like being in love!

Woody Flowers

I've always been drawn to art and creative things. My favorite birthday gift as a child was my Crayola Carousel, so it was no surprise to my mother when I took up scrapbooking. For many years, it was just something I did on the side, never really getting involved in it, until a friend showed me just how artistic it could be. I had found nothing else that combined my love of writing, photography and art so perfectly. Suddenly, it was my passion. My mother never really caught on to that. To her, it was still just this little thing I did. She did not ask to see pages, and her comments on what I showed her stayed in the "how cute" range. That was fine. It's not necessary for everyone to have the same passions. My mother loves my family; she didn't need to love my scrapbooks.

Things stayed like this for a couple of years until my parents decided to serve a mission for our church. They were sent to Japan. All at once, I went from having parents just down the road to having parents halfway around the globe. We coped because we had to. They could e-mail and phone us when they wanted to, so we never missed much.

Scrapbooks became a link to home for my mother. I sent her off with a small scrapbook of all her grandchildren so she could show them off. She loved her brag book. She started telling me about all the people she showed it to— one woman called it a "treasure"—and I loved the feedback. I sent my parents the link to an online gallery where I post my layouts, and Mom loved that, too. Now there was a way she could keep up with my kids, watch them grow and read all the little stories, too. She began to share my talent with others as she sent the link to several women she knew. It was a bit bemusing, actually. Mom was proud of my pages!

About halfway through her time in Japan, she sent me an e-mail just about my scrapbooking. She told me that she thought my pages were beautiful. She could see that I was an artist. Now, my mother is a practical woman, and I had never felt like she really understood my creative side. Through this e-mail I began to see that my mother understood me better than she ever had.

Later, I asked her for some pictures from Japan so I could scrapbook them for an assignment for an online scrapbook store. From the stack of photos she sent me, I chose one simple photo of a little girl in a formal kimono standing outside a shrine. I didn't ask my parents for the journaling; I just wrote about how that sweet photo made me feel and the image it gave me about Japan. I posted it online. Two minutes later, my mother called me. She had been looking at my gallery at the very moment I posted that layout.

"How did you know?" she asked. "You've never been here. How did you know?" She said my words captured exactly how she felt about Japan. That project brought me very close to my mother that day. I felt like not only was she beginning to understand my art better, but I was beginning to understand in some small way what she was doing and why. Since then, there have been other layouts that have brought my mother and me to conversation, tears and laughter, including one about my dad's birthday and the birthday cake we made for him. That one made my dad cry, and it sparked a wonderful conversation about things that we wouldn't have discussed otherwise.

Scrapbooking brought me closer to my parents than I ever thought possible during this time. I have been able to share my life and my art with them over thousands of miles, and in sharing those things, I have shared more of myself. My parents will be home soon, and once again, they will be right down the road. We won't be picking up where we left off before their mission. Thanks to scrapbooking, we'll be closer than that—closer than we would have been had they never left.

Amy R. Brown

Love, Life, Scrapbooking

*All our young lives, we
search for someone to love, someone who
makes us complete. We choose partners
and change partners. We dance to a song
of heartbreak and hope, all the while
wondering if somewhere and somehow
there is someone searching for us.*

From the television series, The Wonder Years

I am a single mom and rarely have time for friendships, romance or even scrapbooking. Between running with the kids and everyday life, sometimes I feel like
life is passing me by. Little did I know that was about to
change.

One day, I was standing in line at a grocery store that
is thirty miles away from the town in which I live. My
two-and-a-half-year-old was fussy and ready to go home,

the cashier was new and kept messing up my order, I was getting a migraine, and I had to get home to get my five-year-old off the bus. Just as I was ready to say "forget it" and walk out, I looked up and saw a man walking into the store. As I looked at him, something inside me clicked, and I realized that it was Dre'. Dre' was the one who got away. I watched him walk around the corner, debated for a minute, then went after him. We hadn't seen each other in seven years, and I knew that he had been in Baghdad fighting the war. I said his name, and he turned around and smiled at me.

He was home on a two-week leave during which we spent every minute together. I showed him my scrapbooks and shared the past seven years of my life with him through pictures. I told him that I would love to do a book for him about his military service. He was thrilled and started collecting pictures. He had to go back to finish his deployment, and we e-mailed, wrote letters and talked on the phone.

When Dre' came home, the sense of relief was overwhelming. He didn't have to go back to his civilian job for a month and a half. We started shopping for supplies for his scrapbook, and the more we shopped, the more he got into the whole scrapbooking idea. We ended up doing his scrapbook together. We scrapped every chance we got. We could scrap up to nine hours at a time. We would laugh and pick on each other's layouts and share ideas. By the time the book was done, I had fallen head over heels in love with him—again. Thank God, he felt the same way. Dre' always says, "Scrapbooking made us bond; it brought us back together."

Doing his scrapbook together made me understand what he went through in Iraq and how important it was for him to be there. Through pictures and lay-outs, the soldiers became real to me. Their hurt, sorrow, fear, loneliness, courage and survival are truly touching. Dre' took his book to one of his drill weekends for the army, and everyone in his unit wants one now. Something as simple as scrapbooking can bring you together, bring pride to your life and share something words aren't always able to express. To my life, it brought love and healing. Although this was our first scrapbook, Dre' and I are planning many more in our life together.

Suzanne Kigler

A "God Thing"

Our truest life is when we are in dreams awake.

Henry David Thoreau

Have you ever done anything major on an impulse and then realized that it could have been a terrible mistake? Here's my impulsive, life-changing move. . . .

I had an acquaintance named Jody. I am calling her an acquaintance because up until three years ago, we were not yet friends. She was the mother in my son's preschool class who always went above and beyond with valentines and party favors. Her children were always dressed adorably, and she had a cute, "pixielike" haircut that only certain people can pull off. She was the epitome of perfect.

Rumor had it that she was interested in opening a scrapbook store in our town. Scrapbooking was a hobby of mine. I was working on several albums, and I was a consultant for an at-home scrapbooking business—just to support my habit.

After hearing the rumor of Jody wanting to open her store for more than six months, I started to think that I might be interested in having something to do with the store, too. I mean, not *own* it or anything, but maybe help.

On a Tuesday night, I was at a crop with some friends. The hot conversation was that Jody was having difficulty getting her store open. No one really knew details; they were just speculating that there were money issues with the start-up costs.

On a Wednesday afternoon, I was driving down a street near her house. Without having any prior thoughts, I picked up my cell phone. I honestly did not know what I would say when she answered. *If her machine answers, I'll just hang up,* I thought.

But Jody answered.

"Hi, Jody," I began. "This is Ami." We exchanged the cordial "how are you" that unfamiliar people typically share. Finally, I said (all in one breath), "I heard that you are thinking about opening a scrapbook store. I don't know what the reasons are that you haven't done it yet, but if it's because you need a partner, think about me."

There, I'd done it. I hadn't thought about it for more than five minutes before I picked up the phone, but I did it. And now there was silence on the line.

Stupid . . . what was I thinking, anyway?

After a long pause, Jody said, "Well, let me talk to my husband about this. I have thought about having a partner, but there are a lot of pros and cons to partners."

Yeah, I thought, *especially partners you barely know.* I tried to put the phone call out of my mind. I figured I would hear from her in a few days, either way.

The next day, my cell phone rang. I didn't recognize the number, but I answered it anyway. It was Jody.

"Is this Ami?"

"Yes."

"This is Jody. Can I just tell you that I have not been able to stop thinking about your phone call since yesterday? I talked to my husband, expecting him to tell me I was crazy, and I talked to my parents, expecting them to tell me I was crazy. But both of them said I should go for it!"

I had to smile because she said all of that in one breath, like I had done the day before.

"Really?" I said with a question.

"Yes." She told me that owning a scrapbook store had always been a dream of hers, and that her family all seemed to agree that maybe this was a "God thing."

We started planning right away. This had all happened in mid-January. By February 1, we held a communitywide crop and announced our plans. Our store opened in April 2003. Early in 2005, we moved our store to a larger location.

Jody and I are now the best of friends. It is truly amazing to me. I am constantly hearing about friends who go into business together and eventually become bitter enemies. Ironically, Jody and I started off barely knowing each other. All I can think of is that we have been successful because our relationship was built on business decisions, rather than emotional decisions that friends would make.

Or maybe Jody's family was right—it really is a "God thing."

Ami Mizell-Flint

The Cards Kept Arriving

Help one another is part of the religion of sisterhood.

Louisa May Alcott

Last summer I watched my wife, Donna, succumb to her battle with cancer. It was a troubling and astonishing journey. It included a wedding anniversary, a road trip and a new understanding of the power of friendship.

This story started a few years ago when Donna became passionate about scrapbooking. She joined an Internet community of scrapbookers, and through this community, Donna became acquainted with a large number of people in Canada, the United States and Australia. They got together in cyberspace to ask questions, share scrapbooking ideas and generally have a good time.

In e-mail and bulletin-board posts, Donna's personality and smile shone through and captivated the people she contacted. Some of them became close friends, sharing silly moments, triumphs and tragedies—even though they had never met in person. Donna became famous in this community because of the extraordinary number and variety of creative scrapbooking ideas she originated, and mostly because she shared all these ideas freely.

Last year, we had no real indication anything was wrong with Donna until June 7. That evening, we were watching TV when my daughter looked at Donna and said, "Mom, you're yellow!" Sure enough, her skin had a yellow pallor, and so did the whites of her eyes. Donna had jaundice. The next day, we went to the family doctor. After a brief examination, he sent us directly to the St. Boniface Hospital emergency department where Donna was immediately admitted. In a couple of hours, we had a preliminary diagnosis of stage IV pancreatic cancer that had metastasized to the liver. Three days later, the diagnosis was confirmed with a median expected survival time of six months. It turned out Donna had less than three months left, and all but nine days of that would be spent in the hospital.

Donna took a very matter-of-fact attitude toward her condition. She knew there was nothing she could do about it, so she avoided dwelling on her illness and focused her attention on her visitors. She was always upbeat and interested in everything new in her visitors' lives.

When the Internet scrapbooking community learned of Donna's illness, they started sending cards through the mail. The cards appeared in groups of two or three or eight each day. They all held personal messages to Donna, wishing her well and describing what she meant to the individual sender. Donna read every card, and her eyes frequently filled with tears while reading the messages.

While in the hospital, Donna suffered through blood clots, the insertion of a stent to open her bile duct, a pulmonary embolism, the insertion of a filter to catch blood clots, several infections, severe vomiting, side effects of chemotherapy and mounting pain as the cancer progressed.

Through all these trials, Donna maintained her composure, sense of humor, sunny smile and unconquerable spirit. She greeted all visitors with a cheerful, "Hi, how are you?" accompanied by her radiant and sincere smile. All of her visitors left feeling better than when they arrived.

And the cards kept arriving.

On August 9, Donna had been in the hospital for almost two months. It was also our twenty-ninth wedding anniversary. We had a decidedly low-key celebration in the hospital.

About a half hour after I left the hospital that evening, a face peeked around the door of Donna's room, then another, then a third. Donna knew who they were. She recognized them from scrapbook layouts they had shared on the Internet, but they had never met in person. Donna just couldn't believe they were here.

These three people—Sherilyn, Stacy and her husband, Darren—had driven from Fort Worth, Texas, to Winnipeg, Canada, just to see Donna.

They stayed well past the end of visiting hours and returned early the next day. When I arrived that morning, they were all chatting away as if they had been meeting like this for years. They stayed for another four hours. Then they headed back to Texas.

They transformed one of our worst wedding anniversaries into one of our best. Donna was thrilled by the visit and enjoyed watching the reaction from subsequent visitors when she told them about the Texans' "road trip."

And the cards kept arriving.

Early in the morning on August 31, Donna lost her battle with cancer.

The road trip and the cards definitely brightened Donna's hospital stay. But they did something else . . . something far more important. Most of us go through life never knowing if the work we do is ever used or appreciated. Donna wondered the same thing about her scrapbooking ideas. The cards and the road trip showed that all of her efforts were being used, appreciated and enjoyed.

In person or over the Internet, this is the incredible power of friendship.

And the cards kept arriving.

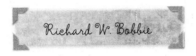

Richard W. Bobbie

Connected to the Past

No one can pass through life, any more than he can pass through a bit of country, without leaving tracks behind, and those tracks may often be helpful to those coming after him in finding their way.

Sir Robert Baden-Powell

It's All About Kinfolk

In every conceivable manner, the family is a link to our past, bridge to our future.

Alex Haley

Growing up, I always knew that family was important. We would spend holidays, birthdays and interspersed weekends with my aunts, uncles and plenty of cousins from both sides of the family. My interest as a child was far more into playing games with my cousins than in listening to the adults talk on and on. My great-aunt Ray would always say in her Southern drawl, "It's all about kinfolk. You remember that, you hear?" My cousins and I would just laugh at "crazy, old" Aunt Ray and run off to play some more.

When I was a teenager, we continued to have extended family gatherings. Most of the cousins still had no interest in stories from the "old days" and would hang out on the front porch listening to music on the transistor radio. My older sister, who was in college at the time, had betrayed the cousins' code by loitering around the adults. You see, she had to do a research paper on genealogy and would sit listening intently to every word that sputtered from the lips of our elders. Okay, so it was kind of neat to hear we had an ancestor who came over on the Mayflower or another ancestor who was beheaded by King Henry VIII for "fooling around" with the queen. We even had a painted plate with the Norris Castle on it—a supposed family castle in England. But still, I would not pay it any attention.

Years went by. Cousins grew up and got married, having children of their own. Great Aunt Ray died at the ripe old age of ninety, and my father died at the young age of fifty-six. I was twenty-seven years old and eight months pregnant with my second child when he died. I think that is when it hit me . . . why didn't I pay attention? Why didn't I listen to the stories about his past? He was taken from me too young, and I wanted to know more about him and his life. After time, my mom had gone through some of my dad's things, sharing them among the five children. I took my pile of papers, photos, and memorabilia and tucked them away for safekeeping. Whenever I came across something else about my dad and his life, I would add it to the mounting mass I had already compiled.

More than ten years had passed when I discovered the hobby of scrapbooking. As I started to create page after page and album after album of my children, I decided it was high time for me to make a heritage album. So I pulled out my stash of photos and memories of my father, joined *Genealogy.com* and started by typing in my name followed by my parents' names and so on. It wasn't long before I was pulling out my baby book and the family Bible to fill in more information about my predecessors. I contacted my sister and sent for a copy of the genealogy report she did for college and called my surviving aunts for more information. I then purchased the computer software "My Family Tree." I worked to the point of having one hundred names in my family tree. I was so entranced with finding my roots and stories from the past.

At the same time, I found out that my younger brother was looking into some past family as well. We compared notes, and the excitement grew! He had located two cousins of my father's that we had never met, and through e-mails we were able to obtain more information about our extended family. I started to reflect this information on the pages of my scrapbook. Looking closer at the photos of family members from the past, I could see the resemblance of my aunts, uncles, cousins, sisters, brothers and my children. I was totally intrigued.

Once I started digging deeper, I found real connections to the past. My great-great-great-grandfather from my father's maternal side (Christian F. Bauman) fought and died during the Civil War in the battle of Antietam. Speaking with my father's cousin, she mentioned that my great-great-grandfather on my father's side owned a fruit mercantile in Jacksonville, Florida, but lost everything in a fire during the early 1900s.

When it was time for me to create a page about my great-great grandfather Edward Rite Norris, I plugged into a search engine on my computer and looked for history on Jacksonville, Florida. I typed away, looking for an old newspaper article about a fire in the early 1900s and was shocked to find how big the event actually was—the whole town burned down!

When my father's older sister died, my cousins gave me a box of old family pictures and ledgers to go through. I was quite pleased when I found more information, leading

me to more and more of my ancestors.
Sharing the excitement with my
extended family at yet another
gathering, I found a link to an
ancestor who fought in the
American Revolution. Well, if I
didn't pay attention to American
history or family history in the
past, I was sure paying attention
now! And, guess what . . . so were
my cousins! Of course, our kids
were off playing in the distance,
rolling their eyes at our constant
chatter of the "old days."

As I continue on my genealogical
search for more family members linking us to the past, I can't help but
remember the wise words of my great-
aunt Ray, "It's all about kinfolk." Perhaps
she wasn't so crazy after all.

Allison Connors

READER/CUSTOMER CARE SURVEY

REFG

We care about your opinions! Please take a moment to fill out our online Reader Survey at **http://survey.hcibooks.com**.

As a **"THANK YOU"** you will receive a **VALUABLE INSTANT COUPON** towards future book purchases as well as a **SPECIAL GIFT** available only online! Or, you may mail this card back to us and we will send you a copy of our exciting catalog with your valuable coupon inside.

(PLEASE PRINT IN ALL CAPS)

First Name _____ MI. _____ Last Name _____

Address _____ Email _____

City _____

State _____ Zip _____

1. Gender
- ❑ Female ❑ Male

2. Age
- ❑ 8 or younger
- ❑ 9-12 ❑ 13-16
- ❑ 17-20 ❑ 21-30
- ❑ 31+

3. Did you receive this book as a gift?
- ❑ Yes ❑ No

4. Annual Household Income
- ❑ under $25,000
- ❑ $25,000 - $34,999
- ❑ $35,000 - $49,999
- ❑ $50,000 - $74,999
- ❑ over $75,000

5. What are the ages of the children living in your house?
- ❑ 0 - 14 ❑ 15+

6. Marital Status
- ❑ Single
- ❑ Married
- ❑ Divorced
- ❑ Widowed

7. How did you find out about the book?
(please choose one)
- ❑ Recommendation
- ❑ Store Display
- ❑ Online
- ❑ Catalog/Mailing
- ❑ Interview/Review

8. Where do you usually buy books?
(please choose one)
- ❑ Bookstore
- ❑ Online
- ❑ Book Club/Mail Order
- ❑ Price Club (Sam's Club, Costco's, etc.)
- ❑ Retail Store (Target, Wal-Mart, etc.)

9. What subject do you enjoy reading about the most?
(please choose one)
- ❑ Parenting/Family
- ❑ Relationships
- ❑ Recovery/Addictions
- ❑ Health/Nutrition
- ❑ Christianity
- ❑ Spirituality/Inspiration
- ❑ Business Self-help
- ❑ Women's Issues
- ❑ Sports

10. What attracts you most to a book?
(please choose one)
- ❑ Title
- ❑ Cover Design
- ❑ Author
- ❑ Content

TAPE IN MIDDLE; DO NOT STAPLE

Chicken Soup for the Soul®
3201 SW 15th Street
Deerfield Beach FL 33442-9875

FOLD HERE

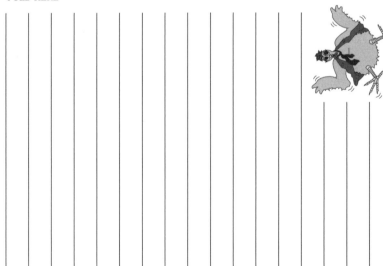

Do you have your own Chicken Soup story
that you would like to send us?
Please submit at: **www.chickensoup.com**

Comments

How I Wish My Grandmother Had Been a Scrapbooker

Time flies over us, but leaves its shadow behind.

Nathaniel Hawthorne

How I wish my grandmother had been a scrapbooker. I never knew my grandmother; she died before I was born, when my mom was just eighteen years old. She had a long battle with breast and bone cancer and passed away in her forties. Afterward, the family scattered to the four winds. It was as if the very fabric that held them together had unraveled.

I didn't know her, but I do know that she liked to take pictures. One day I was looking through some old photos and found one of my great-uncle. Also in the photo was the shadow of a woman, obviously the photographer. On the back of the photo was some handwriting that looks a lot like my own, explaining that the picture was taken on the back porch of the house, and she had "spoiled" the shot by getting her shadow in it. How I love this photo, not so much for the picture itself, but to see the words written on the back. Finding this was the closest I ever felt to knowing my grandmother. Those were her words, her handwriting; it was as if she was speaking to me through time.

If only my grandmother had been a scrapbooker, how I would treasure those albums! I would have wanted her to scrapbook about everything, not just how she felt about her kids, but her hopes, dreams, travels, special events, friends, wedding day, birthday parties, favorite things and her heroic struggle with cancer. How I would so love to read her story, understand the everyday joys and sorrows of her life. I would pore over those albums, savoring every documented moment of a person I never knew, but so wish I could have. And I would hold every single one of those details close to my heart.

Whenever I think of skipping my journaling or assume that a topic is too mundane to scrapbook about, I think of my grandmother. And while I don't need scrapbooks for my grandmother to feel real to me, I would so treasure having more than a few photos, a figure in the shadows of time and a snippet of handwriting.

How I wish my grandmother had been a scrapbooker.

Christine Stoneman

Our Heritage

Reprinted by permission of Mack Dobbie ©2005.

I Scrap for My Mother

Children and mothers never truly part—bound in the beating of each other's heart.

Charlotte Gray

Some people wax poetic about how they are scrapbooking for the many generations to come. With a faraway look in their eyes, they go on and on in their imaginations and out loud about how little "Sally the Fourth" will one day look up on her shelves in her "spacehouse" and read with reverence and honor the scrapbook her great-grandmother lovingly handmade, as she sniffs a tear and glances at the holographic photo of Granny, smiling for eternity, frozen in a 3-D image.

Not me. I mean, sure, I would love future generations to revere what I do; I put a lot of time into each and every layout, and while I am not wild about the thought of a holographic representation of my hind end, I would love my children's children to cherish my books. I am afraid, though, that I am a realist. Things happen to books, even with the best of care and the most honorable of intentions.

I have lost everything I own in a move, so I know that no matter how careful, how "safe" I try to keep them, my scrapbooks might be ruined beyond repair, lost, stolen or have other unforeseen things happen to them. While I cannot say I am okay with that, I am at peace with that possibility. We do not have control over all of our lives, and for that, I am truly grateful. I will do my best, but even my best is left in the hands of God.

So if I am not scrapbooking for "future generations" alone, who am I doing this for? Certainly not just for my four boys. I hope they will one day love my work, but honestly, they are too "in the moment" to care about scrapbooks, and I hope they always live life with such reverence for the here and now. I don't want them worrying too much about tomorrow, other than to be aware that their actions affect the future, and I certainly do not want them dwelling in the past, living on old glories.

The reason I scrapbook is for a woman who was my best friend, my mentor, my muse and my inspiration for life. It is for my mother, Connie Lindquist. She was a pretty remarkable woman, in an ordinary way. She loved baseball, travel, kids, the piano, sand dunes and art. She gave me my love of life and often reminded me never to lose it. I have a scrapbook she made when she was a young adult, several years of Detroit Tiger memorabilia and articles from the 1950s. These things, along with a baseball signed by every member of the Tigers from the 1958 team, are counted among my most valued possessions. I am not a huge baseball fan, but I appreciate the care and love she placed in her work, her book of memories. They give me a glimpse into the woman I loved so very much and honor to this day.

I scrap for my mom. You probably have a clue, if you

have read this far, that I am speaking of her in the past tense. My mother is no longer with us, killed in a tragic accident when I was only six-teen. I still fight, to this day, to come to grips with the pain of her loss. So if she is not here, how can I scrap for her? When I am creating a layout of my four boys or sweet husband, I remember my mother. She had an amazing sense of humor. I try, in my mind, to make her laugh. She also had an appreciation for simple moments. I clearly remember her stroking my hair as she spoke on the phone, one of my favorite childhood memories. I try to capture those kinds of uncomplicated, loving moments with my boys when I take photos to scrap. I journal to my mother . . . she is my audience. If I can, in my imagination, engage her, give her a smile or a small tear, then I know I have the page "right" and am satisfied with it.

Is it hard "selling" to an audience who I can no longer hear or see? No. It makes me feel very much attached to her in a way that I have not been able to connect to her memory before. I think about her words, her insight, her feelings, and I feel close to her once again. When I scrap to my mother, the years without her melt away. She is here, and we can do all the things together that we have missed out on. She can watch my boys grow with me and marvel at how amazing my children are—as amazing, I suspect, as I was to her. I can tell her about my hard days because I remember the days she got frustrated with being a mom. I can tell her about wanting to be

a fantastic mother, but also wanting something "for Nancy," and I remember that she understands because of conversations we had about her returning to work after staying home with her children for many years.

Someday, maybe my boys will remember me and my legacy by "doing things with Mom" even after I am gone, but even if they don't, even if they never open my scrapbooks or cherish my work, even if my scrapbooks go up in a ball of flames tomorrow, the time I have spent on them has not been wasted. By connecting with my mother's memory through my work, I have united myself to all the generations that have come before me. The words, phrases and laughter passed down verbally to me are now captured in my journaling, my sense of balance and my design. I suspect there is more of my mother and her mother before her than I will ever know in the work I do today, linking me to time past and time to come.

Nancy Ann Liedel

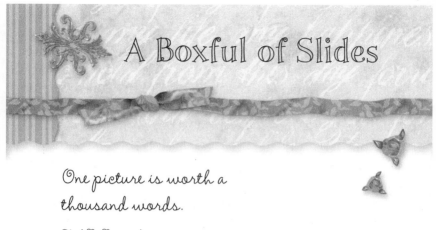

A Boxful of Slides

One picture is worth a thousand words.

Fred R. Barnard

Since I started scrapbooking six years ago, I have been totally addicted. It goes beyond just being a hobby for me—it is an official obsession! What I didn't realize is how this craft could enrich my life. It has been an awesome blessing for me because it has brought me closer to my dad.

My dad passed away eleven years ago. Dad was a fantastic photographer and passed the love of photography on to me—it was something we shared. After Dad died, my mom gave me all of his old slides. Many of my childhood memories were contained on these slides. I rushed out and bought a scanner that could scan slides and saved them in photo format. I spent many afternoons sitting by the computer scanning away. Each scan brought to life wonderful recollections.

My final project was to scan slides from when my dad was in the army in Germany. This was when he was young, before he met my mom. I wasn't looking forward to the slides that awaited me. I was saddened that I hadn't taken the time when Dad was alive to sit and listen to his army experiences. He happened to have met one of his lifelong friends in the army. His name is Bill. Bill and his family shared many holidays and summer vacations with our family, so I knew I would recognize him in the photos, but I wasn't sure I would know anything else about the people and places in these pictures.

All the army slides were stored in slide trays (twenty-five to thirty slides in each), and all the trays were in a metal box. As I opened the metal box I found twelve trays labeled neatly with the date. *Well, at least I will know the dates*, I thought to myself. I pulled out the first tray and sadness flooded my heart. I took off the top and there was a piece of paper folded, lying inside. I opened the paper and it was in my dad's handwriting. Tears welled up in my eyes; I couldn't read the words my dad had left behind. After gaining my composure, I perused the words to find it was a numbered list of each slide telling me where and who was in each picture. I couldn't believe my eyes. It was like Dad was there telling me about each slide! I quickly ripped off the lids to the other eleven boxes, and there was a letter in each one. Some were handwritten in his quirky penmanship, and others were typed. My heart

filled with joy. He had written these letters to my grandmother so she could look at the slides he would send
home to her; she was able to experience his travels, too!

After scanning all the slides and reading all of his captions, I had so many questions. I knew that Bill, his friend
from so many years ago, was my only hope. I called him
one Sunday afternoon, and he filled in all the gaps for me.
I e-mailed Bill photos from time to time, and he in turn
told me great stories of the adventures he and my dad had
in their old VW bug they bought in Germany. Now I am
putting all those pictures, captions and stories into a
scrapbook about Dad. His story was not lost after all; it
was just contained in a boxful of slides.

Karen Flanigan

Reunion Group Scrapbook

Go back. Go back in time.
Everyone's life is a chain of memories.
In each chain there are shining links,
happenings where this element of wonder
. . . was very strong. Why don't you reach
out and relive some of those memories?

Arthur Gordon

One of the ever-popular themes of scrapbooking is school memories, but usually these are books made by a parent for a child. Our schooldays scrapbook was made by—and for—a bunch of midlife baby boomers! You see, about ten years ago, a group of us became reconnected after our thirtieth class reunion. Our Reunion Group gets together once a month, and we have become the closest of friends again, just like we were in high school, junior-high school and even grade school!

Of course, the first thing school friends do is drag out that great memory preserver, a.k.a. the high-school yearbook. We had a huge laugh while looking through it, and it took us on a long walk down memory lane. As we got to talking, we decided it would be neat to create a Reunion Group Memory Book. Since Stephanie was the first to be enrolled in scrapbooking classes, she was elected to guide us through the project.

Coming up with a color theme was a piece of cake because we used our school colors: purple and gold. Our mascot was a hornet, so hornets and bees adorn nearly every page. (We opted for nice bees, not mean-looking ones!)

Thanks to copy machines, we were able to enlarge those tiny black-and-white photos from our yearbooks. Then my friends (and their moms) dug through photo albums to find pictures from slumber parties, birthday parties, Girl Scout events, school plays and those grade-school group pictures. Of course, we included plenty of current photos of how we look now. We even have a group photo from our fortieth class reunion! (We were the best-looking and youngest-looking ones there. Ha!)

Humor surfaced right off the bat as we remembered silly junior-high nicknames, like Peaches, Pickles, Petunia and Pammie-Poo. (I am NOT making those names up!) The inscriptions classmates wrote in each girl's yearbook provided plenty of funny and corny material, too: "2 cute + 2 be = 4 gotten"; "You're a cute girl but a little silly" (signed Pammie-Poo!); and "To my best friend and the cleanest person I've ever known" (we never could figure out what that meant).

Poignant and sad memories joined the humorous ones. When Kristi went through breast-cancer treatments last

year, we made a lap quilt for her that featured embroi-
dered hearts with each girl's signature. Fabric swatches
from that quilt are next to photos of Kristi holding it.

It's trite, but we just had to include before-and-after pictures of each of us. How different (yet similar) we look!
The schoolgirl with a ponytail and freckles on her nose is
now a woman who still has freckles, although the ponytail
has been replaced with a stylish banana-clip. The girl in
those awful black-rimmed glasses is now spectacle-free
because of laser surgery. Of course, some of us have
picked up a few extra pounds in forty years, but we won't
even talk about that!

What a treasure trove of memories
we rediscovered—photos of school
friends who have since died, favorite
teachers, old beaus and former "best
friends for life" that we've completely
lost track of.

Of course, the purpose of scrapbooking
is to preserve memories, and the Reunion
Group scrapbook is chock-full of memories.
One of our best memories, however, isn't within the covers of the book. It's the memory of the very act of creating
this scrapbook—the very best of friends sitting around a
kitchen table with scissors, glue and a plate of warm
chocolate-chip cookies. Good memories should always be
preserved because, like good friends, they are forever.

Donna Rogers

Just One Scrapbook

Through family history we discover the most beautiful tree in the forest of creation—our family tree. Its numerous roots reach back through history, and its branches extend throughout eternity.

J. Richard Clarke

In the wee hours of a hot summer night, after I'd spent four grueling hours on the highways with a wailing baby in the backseat, I sat slumped over a conference room table in a cramped hotel room. I was begging my husband, with my eyes, to "Let's get out of here," when in burst Aunt Emma (married into the family) with an old tattered, dusty, moldy-smelling leather scrapbook under her arm. She plopped the scrapbook down on the table in front of me and said in her high-pitched voice, "Here, I thought you might want this. It's been in my basement for years, and I was about to throw it away!" Immediately I thought, *Oh gosh . . . another boring family reunion looking at scrapbooks and listening to my father tell stories.*

I looked at her bleary-eyed as I nursed my baby and casually flipped open the book. I'd seen only one other scrapbook with black pages like this, and that was at my grandmother's house when I was a child. Well . . . this album happened to be her grandmother's scrapbook. As I tried to turn the pages while still nursing my baby, every page crumbled under the weight of the photographs, newspaper clippings and telegrams. The photos were mostly of African-American people from the early 1900s, and there wasn't anything written down. No names, no dates, no captions . . . nothing. Now, this was something I'd never seen before.

As others started looking on with me, Aunt Emma explained that it was her mother-in-law's scrapbook, my great-grandma Josephine, who died in the early 1970s at the age of one hundred. The more Aunt Emma talked, the more my adrenaline pumped. Where I was once sleepy and irritable, I was now wide awake. I passed off my sleeping baby to my mother because my dad (the first scrapbooker I ever knew) and I were almost fighting over the book. I was fascinated by the sepia tones, the early 1900 clothing, the foxed pages, even the mold and mildew. My mind desperately wanted to know, *Who were these black folks, and how could they afford to have photographs taken so soon after the end of slavery?* My heart leaped at the possibility that all of these people were family members.

My grandmother and a few of her siblings recognized some of the unnamed people in the photographs. Of course, they recognized themselves in school photos, their parents (during their courting days) and even some World War II telegrams. However, this was my first time seeing Grandma Josephine as a young mother, just like myself. I'd always thought of her as a frail, little old woman.

Unfortunately, my grandmother and my other great aunts and uncles couldn't identify many people in the photos. *Not to worry,* I thought, *Aunt Elsie will be arriving tomorrow, and she'll tell me who everyone is.*

You see, Aunt Elsie is the last living sibling of my great-grandfather and daughter of Great-Grandma Josephine, although she was in her late eighties. I hoped she would be able to answer all my questions about the unidentified folks in Grandma's scrapbook. I stayed up all night poring over the album. I wondered, *Who are all those beautiful brown faces staring back at me, and, most importantly, how are they connected to my great-grandma? Why did she so lovingly keep them in this album . . . and why had newspaper clippings been used as background paper?*

Morning arrived, and I was waiting for the local office supply store to open its doors. I couldn't let everyone keep looking at this album; I had to try to preserve this scrapbook in its original state. The album was so fragile it was literally falling apart with every turn of a page. I asked the salesclerk to color-copy every page twice—a copy for me and one for my dad. The salesclerk assisting me was just as fascinated with the photos. A few hundred dollars later, I was off to the family reunion to quiz Aunt Elsie.

Aunt Elsie arrived, looking as spry as ever. In fact, she was in better health than the daughter-in-law who was caring for her. After all of the formalities, I finally got Aunt Elsie alone to look at the album. I was bubbling over with excitement and anticipation. I had my little acid-free, fade-proof pen, ready to write down everything she said. I just knew she'd be able to identify everyone because she had grown up with the album, right? Hadn't she lived with Grandma Josephine during the time this album was being compiled. Surely Grandma had told her all the stories surrounding the people and the events in the photos . . .

As Aunt Elsie grinned and slowly looked at the photos (without eyeglasses I might add), we got to the end of the album, but she could identify only her mother and herself in a few photos. Boy, was I heartbroken! Just when I thought the window to my past would be opened and I'd know everything I ever wanted to know about my great-grandmother . . . SLAM, the window was shut. To date, all I knew about Grandma Josephine was that she raised a brood of children in a small rural town south of Pittsburgh, Pennsylvania, and was strong in her faith. Now I was left with even more questions than ever.

It was at that moment, as a new mother, that I vowed that my kids, grandkids and great-grandkids would know who I was and that I'd write everything down in a scrapbook. Well, that was in 1996. I spent the next two years gathering photographs from any family member who would part with them long enough for me to make copies. That effort led to over fifty volumes of family heirlooms.

For the past nine years I have spent every single day "living and breathing" scrapbooking. I sold scrapbook supplies, bought thousands of dollars worth of supplies, taught classes, held crops, coordinated multiple family reunions and even hired genealogists to unlock the secrets of my ancestors. I was determined that my children would know right away why they all had on matching outfits, and they would know how to do head-stone rubbings. Now my five children know without fail that every family trip will involve a stop at a scrapbook store and maybe a cemetery. My father and I share this new obsession. Like thousands of other scrapbookers, we are known as "addicts" and dare anyone to ever throw away a photograph or, worse yet, put one in a scrapbook without writing something down. One thing's for sure: I bet no one would ever believe that such a new purpose-driven lifestyle would emerge from just one scrapbook.

Lisa M. Sanford

The Power of a Book

A good book is the precious lifeblood of a master spirit, embalmed and treasured up on purpose to a life beyond life.

John Milton

There I was at our homeschool used curriculum sale. I had my booth set up with our discarded books, as well as scrapbook inventory I was trying to get rid of that day. As the sale was drawing to a close, I finally got a chance to look around at other people selling items, and there I found it . . . a book I was given as a prize in second grade!

First of all, I don't normally "win" things. This is one of the few things I can say I actually won in my life, and this wasn't just any book. It was a book titled *The 50 States* and was put out by *National Geographic*. The book was written for children and was in a style similar to Dorling Kindersley (DK) books today. It contained almost three hundred twelve-by-twelve-inch pages filled with great color photos, small bits of information with pictures (state bird, flower and capital), as well as pages of information for further reading, and each state had a map. There are these really cool maps with transparency overlays, one showing a view of the United States from outer space, then an overlay transparency showing the weather patterns. Another one shows proper growth and development of a city. The best part, the back of the book, had a pocket for a map. The map included was a full-color wall map of the United States.

The memories flooded back as I spent nearly twenty minutes going through this book. As a child it was my prized possession. I remembered winning it; I remember lying on my bed looking through page after page of information . . . playing with the transparency maps, folding and unfolding the wall map. I think both my sister and I used that book for at least a dozen reports. Eventually we both outgrew it, and so it went the way of all our old books onto Mom's school shelf. (Mom is a public school teacher.) The only problem with that is that her "cool" books had a tendency of walking away, never to be seen again; thus the story of my United States book. Yet now here it was before me again after twenty-four years. I felt nine years old again, reliving my excitement.

As I drove home with my newfound treasure, I kept thinking about this book and why it held such power over me. I surprised myself with my answer. This book had all the makings of a great scrapbook (and this was created way before scrapbooking was on the scene)—great pictures, wonderful "bits" of journaling about the pictures, current embellishments (how many of you have scrapped with transparencies?) But more so, this book held memories . . . memories of being the envy of the class when I won it. Memories of the endless hours I spent reading it. Memories of childhood reports and games played with "the map." Most of all, memories of it bringing me a bit closer to places I couldn't go.

Then I started realizing that I hold this same power when I scrapbook. The pictures I take, the comments I make—all tell a story about those I love and hold dear. I love watching the kids relive their baseball games and birthday parties. Seeing their excitement and hearing the "Oh, that was the present Josiah gave me" and "Do you remember that pop fly I caught, ending the inning?" I love being able to share my children's lives with my parents, knowing I can show them something they wouldn't have a chance to see otherwise. Someday when my children are older, I hope they will be able to once again relive those memories and truly understand the "power of a book"—a book that will hold them captive and spellbound as they turn the pages, each photo causing them to relive their childhood. Until then, I have the joy of knowing I am the one who is creating that book.

Betsy Burnett

A Scrapper's Perspective

*Grandmothers are voices of the
past and role models of the present.*

Unknown

She lived a long, hard life. She lived through two world wars . . . one as a child and one as a woman.

After her beloved husband went to war, she lived for many years without knowing that he was still alive, locked away in a prison camp. She survived her own war of poverty by digging for food in abandoned gardens.

She lived through the deaths of two of her children. She lived faithfully through trials and tribulations when so many might have given up. And yet, she lived a good life.

She was my grandmother. She was proud. She was strong. She was a survivor. She was full of memories . . . until she was robbed of them by Alzheimer's disease.

My grandmother lived through things most can probably never even imagine. She lived in a world where a woman had a set role in life. She lived in a world where domesticity was an art one dared not to master. She lived in a world where women were not always equal to men. She lived in a world in which most could never survive.

And, sadly, I'll likely never know much more than that. I am sorry that I discovered the world of scrapbooking so long after she passed away, because looking back now, there are so many things I would ask her.

I would ask her what it felt like to listen to the sound of planes dropping bombs overhead while she cradled her children in her arms. I would ask her how she stayed so strong in a world that for her was so often uncertain.

I would even ask her about the more trivial things. Who taught her how to mend socks with those little wooden eggs? In this throwaway day and age, that's a concept we just don't have. What exactly were all those yummy recipes whose aromas would fill her house every Saturday morning?

Looking back, I wish I'd captured little details that are now just distant memories. I remember her bathroom vanity with all the little vials and bottles. But I can't remember what was inside them. I remember that she'd read the paper . . . but I can't remember which section she'd turn to first.

So many missed memories . . . .

I won't let it happen again. However it came about, whether by some divine force or by mere happenstance, I have discovered an art that is not only fun and whimsical, but meaningful and poignant. I have discovered an art that I will never give up, an art I don't see falling out of favor anytime soon.

Our scrapbooks can document and preserve our most precious memories. Some are silly and whimsical. Some are somber and melancholy. Most are fleeting. All are priceless!

Jennifer Howland

Sentimental Old Fool

Memories are like keepsakes
. . . always to be treasured.

Author Unknown

usting—still not a favorite chore in my seventies, but my hay fever, not my housekeeping, reminds me every week it's that time again. I picked up my dust cloth and was wiping off precious grandchild fingerprints when a whim told me to open the doors of the big, square end table. My beloved scrapbooks of greetings and treasures stood on end in perfect annual sequence, some bulging and some overflowing. Loose and homeless mementos fairly warned that if I should cram one more item within, I'd be sorry.

Right in front and quite alone, a beauty of a card from our wedding anniversary caught my eye. The silken cover and lovely wishes penned by a dear one turned on a sudden trickle of tears. I tucked it into the anniversary book and began touching and reading more sentiments created by the Hallmarks of the world. What sweet reminders of our decades in all their vibrant phases. Yes, Ken and I had cherished a fifty-year ride that hadn't even been a thought or dream when we fell in love at first sight. *What a nice feeling to have never had regret,* I thought to myself. A well-meaning friend had warned me that she had never had "words" with her husband. I rather bluntly responded that I wouldn't give any marriage a snowball's chance in heck without "words." Her marriage eventually failed, while mine remained on track, words and all.

Running my sleeve across my cheeks, I plunked down on the floor to read random selections from somewhere in time. I toppled the stack of scrapbooks and pulled an ancient one from the bottom. There were Ken's generic letters reminding me of our youthful and torrid romance. That was a mistake. He was born devoid of even one single love letter bone. I haven't the faintest idea what it was that kept him from setting his feelings on paper. Privacy was his middle name, but oh how I wished he had been a schmaltzy card and posy guy. I giggled aloud while wedging the letters back into their decorated envelope. One day the kids and grandchildren will groan in frustration that we didn't gush romance in every line.

A little worse for wear, there appeared a book bursting with napkins, programs and colorful paper greetings. Many were for me on Mother's Days, birthdays and valentines from our children. What fun to note their changes in handwriting and the sudden personal loving words not prompted by a teacher. A few backward crayoned letters conveyed their own precious thoughts in a way no mom could forget. And yet, I had. I had forgotten the little poems and sayings encircled with bright paper flowers and rainbows. I recounted aloud their newsy messages from Brownie camp, college and basic training until, alas, my face grew hot while sentimental tears rained into my lap.

As if ghostly visions were hovering over me, I smiled and passed over a dreary scrapbook of sympathies. My afternoon was turning into a rush of pent-up emotions. Even though the release was leaving me contentedly fulfilled, I couldn't bring myself to view so many kindly respects. I sat quietly for a moment, sipping tea and reflecting on the beloved mother and father who had adopted me over seventy years before. I needed to write more of their love story and our three lives together, a legacy only a few are privy to. Someday soon, I promised myself. All twelve grandchildren should hear about it.

An old-fashioned leather book appeared from another place and another time. It contained tintypes and ragged-edged black-and-white photographs of my biological ancestors, a precious keepsake from a new and loving half-brother. How odd these ancients looked, seated and standing so stiffly, as though the slightest breeze would do them in. Dark clothes, long tresses done up in buns and ever-present stoic features seemed to distinguish none from the rest of the world. A faded blue, flowered thank-you note with fancy script fell to the floor. It was dated June 4, 1847. I sighed at the wonder of it, still in one piece. The natural mother I had searched for, well after the death of my parents, had sent me a raft of cards and pictures. We two redheaded peas in a pod sit side-by-side in small twin frames in my den. She died just before our first meeting, unselfishly and unknowingly sending her son to our San Francisco reunion in her place.

A special red scrapbook seemed to beckon me. It looked unfamiliar somehow, and it's no wonder. It contained pressed flowers of pure love and hope from a time I preferred to forget. Yet I had saved each and every precious card while in the hospital after a ghastly accident took my arm at sixty-three. Encouraging notes meant the world to me after being sent to arm and hand surgeons across the state. Childlike homesickness had surfaced mightily once again during the long ordeal. Dear nurses spent many moments tenderly decorating my room with plush animals from a loving church family, none of whom knew me from Adam in that strange city. God had worked in wondrous and mysterious ways those eight weeks.

I shivered while confronting three manila envelopes of condolences, some from folks I never knew, but they knew my husband. Just then it didn't seem necessary to remind myself of the recent agonizing year suffered by my beloved. I felt my face flush and tried hard to hold the flood back. Sometime soon I'll pick out a lovely scrapbook to save the sentiments and the pictorial story of this grand family's scattering of Pop's ashes atop our mountain.

Suddenly it was five o'clock, and I hadn't even thought about dinner. Instead, I was tear-stained and as stiff as a new broom from sitting cross-legged among my memories. What déjà vu it had been, and what a well-dusted, tidy cupboard I returned the newly organized albums to. I had reviewed and refreshed pieces of my youth and adulthood that had dwelled long in that place. More than fifty years of the good, a few of the bad, and it felt terrific, for this had been a life, and a good one at that. I promised myself I would view and paste again soon before another fifty years rolls by. I must hurry!

Kathe Campbell

From the Heart

A good heart
is better than all
the heads in
the world.

Edward Bulwer-Lytton

Before "Scrapbook" Was a Verb

Sooner or later we all discover that the important moments in life are not advertised ones, not the birthdays, the graduations, the weddings, not the great goals achieved. The real milestones are less prepossessing. They come to the door of memory.

Susan B. Anthony

Some of the events of our lives cannot be expressed adequately in words. The joy of your wedding day is one. While words alone can't recapture the emotions of the day, I was to learn some of the thrill can be relived by simple gestures.

When Jim and I set the date of June 30, 1967, and began our wedding plans, I started a scrapbook. In it I put brochures of china, crystal and silver patterns we had selected, along with the glossy paper inserts that described our everyday tableware. If there was a party or shower, I gave the event a special page in my scrapbook. There I taped the invitation, the guest list and the newspaper clipping detailing the festivity. I kept all the notes from well-wishers and place cards from the table settings, pressed the corsages I was given at each event, and posted photographs we had taken or ones someone else took and shared with us. I spent many late-night and early-morning hours thumbing through this collection of mementos. At the time it was just something fun to do. How could I have known what a treasure it would become!

Society gives certain anniversaries more attention than others. Personally, I feel the merit of each one, whether it's our first or our twenty-first, as each year brings to our marriage new memories and deeper meaning. We celebrated most of our anniversaries in a quiet, subdued way. Usually a card or mutual gift, like lawn furniture, was enough to honor the day.

As our twenty-fifth anniversary approached, however, even I felt that I wanted to do something very special for this one. I wanted somehow to share that time of our life with those who had helped us in so many ways to make our day special. You know how it is with time, though. Friends and family move away, and getting together gets harder. Besides, how many of our friends and family would even remember that time as clearly as we did? But the thought occurred to me that even if those friends and family didn't share all the vivid memories, each one surely would remember what they had done for us. I went to the closet in the hallway. On the top shelf I kept our wedding pictures, my bride's book, what little china and crystal we had, the silver trays and bowls, and my scrapbook. I pulled out the scrapbook, sat on the floor in the hallway with my back against the wall and once again thumbed through the pages. I'm not sure why it is called a scrapbook, but today I thought of how these scraps were more than just yellowed, brittle pieces of newspaper, faded cards and overdried flowers with net and ribbon attached. They had become the centerpieces, scraps if you will, of the quilt of my life. Where I was today had started and grown from here.

I pulled out every newspaper clipping, invitation and significant reminder of anyone related to our wedding—those who had given showers, parties or teas; bridesmaids; groomsmen; preacher; piano player and soloist; everyone I could find. I made photocopies of each selection.

I purchased some note cards with "Thank You" embossed on the front in silver letters. The inside was blank. I took them to a printer and had this message printed inside:

6/30/92

Dear One,

   You may not remember where you were on this date twenty-five years ago, but we do—and we want to again thank you for helping to make that an unforgettable day for us.

                    Fondly and in celebration of our
                    Silver Wedding Anniversary

With each note we enclosed the copy of their invitation, newspaper article or photo and sent our love and gratitude to them once again, twenty-five years later.

It was a wonderful ongoing celebration! Preparing the notes released a flood of memories of that time of our life. The days that followed brought phone calls and visits from each note recipient. We laughed and recalled everything we could remember about each event.

This simple gesture had allowed us to recapture the excitement and spirit of our wedding day, and it was all possible because of an unknown treasure from twenty-five years ago—my scrapbook.

Andy Skidmore

The Cartoon Stick People Family

Every child deserves a home of his own.

Harry Holt

W hen it came time for my husband and I to begin to think about having a family, the obvious choices did not seem to be as clear as it did for most couples. Yes, we could proceed down the path of the traditional family beginnings of pregnancy, but somehow that did not seem like the right approach for us. We knew there were lots of children who needed a good home, and that information consumed our hearts and minds. We began to explore adoption and found that path was an intersection with many directions—independent, domestic, international and special needs. After years of struggling with the decision of how to start our family, we decided on the special-needs path; though possibly rocky and treacherous, it was the right path for us.

We completed the required training, background screens, home studies and much more to become approved. The entire process from the moment we reached our decision to receiving our approved status took almost one year. Now the hard part began—finding the right child or children for us.

The waiting and searching were emotionally painful. We wanted so much to have a child to love. We would dream about the things we would do together and how our lives would be different—better. We had a wonderful caseworker who kept us informed about the children available and the process. We were told our first meeting would be short—maybe an hour—and would include our caseworker, and the child and his/her caseworker.

We dreamed about that meeting, but wondered about how we would be able to learn about this child—likes, dislikes, things he or she liked to do—in only one hour. We knew if that meeting went well, we would have more visits, but this could possibly be the most important hour of our lives. We needed to decide how it should go so that we could learn about the child and the child could learn about us. We wanted the child to choose us as much as we were given the opportunity to choose. Again, one hour was the challenge. We had so many questions: What are your favorite foods? Do you like school? One day the answer became clear—spend the hour talking about the child and create our story in a scrapbook.

Our direction now determined, I quickly became a scrapbooking fan. My husband took the pictures, while I crafted the pages. There would be a page on each of us doing everyday things. There were pictures of my husband mowing grass and sitting in his favorite chair. There were pictures of me planting flowers and, of course, working on the scrapbook. We added a page on our dog, our house and the child's bedroom. Then we began working on the story of our extended family—the child's hopefully soon-to-be grandparents, aunts, uncles, cousins, friends and neighbors.

We created pages on our local school, church and community. Telling the story of present day was easy; now we were faced with how to share the dream of our future together. I decided on cartoon stick people. The cartoon stick people in our scrapbook went on vacation and did fun family things together. The scrapbook was capped off with a letter from us. Finally, our story was captured in our scrapbook.

Almost ten months after we were approved, a child became available for adoption who seemed perfect for us. She was fourteen and needed a good home. The more we learned about her through our caseworker, the more excited we became. On the day of our first visit, we were almost rendered speechless as our caseworker, and by now one of our dearest friends, drove us to the restaurant to meet quite possibly our future daughter.

We got there very early, probably because I was so nervous that I incorrectly gauged the time and distance. Our plan was to leave the scrapbook in the car, and if all went well, we would then bring it out. Because of her age and the disappointments she had already experienced, we were prepared for anything. A move to live with us would mean leaving behind her school, teachers and friends to start all over in a new place. This is a very hard decision for anyone, but at fourteen, when friends are very important, to think about going to live with complete strangers—well, we knew she would be conflicted to say the least.

When she walked into the restaurant, I froze. My husband put his hand on my shoulder to steady me or possibly to steady himself. We all nervously sat at a large table. Our nervousness quickly fell away to busy chatter. Our one-hour session grew into two hours. When someone realized the time, we knew we would have to leave soon. Our caseworker kept giving me the thumbs-up sign under the table. I knew she was very pleased at how well this meeting had gone.

As we began to exchange phone numbers and set a time to speak, our caseworker went to the car to get the scrapbook. She brought it in and gave it to me. I presented it and explained its purpose. She opened it with such care. Even though we were over our time limit and our caseworker had other engagements, no one would interrupt her and allowed her to study each page. As the visit ended, she cradled the scrapbook in her arms as we watched them walk to their car.

Shortly thereafter, we began our visits. First, it was for a day, and then we worked up to a weekend. Because this would be a tough transition for her, we took things very slowly. On one of our early visits, she asked if I would help her create a scrapbook of her life. I was so pleased to find this was something we could do together. We spread out the few pictures she had of foster families she had lived with, and we began to put them together. As her school was nearing the end of the term and the plan was for her to move in with us for the summer, we gave her a camera to take pictures of her school, teachers and friends. Memories are important for everyone.

Once again we are dreaming of cartoon stick people on scrapbook pages. Big ones or little ones, girls or boys— who knows what the future cartoon stick person will be. But one thing is for sure—that cartoon stick person will be loved.

Lorie Couch

Scraps of Love

Charity from the heart brings joy.

The Bratzlaver

I am a passionate scrapbooker. I love to take pieces of paper, pictures and stories to preserve and pass along precious memories. However, it is an expensive hobby, and although I wanted to have a scrapbook club after school, I had no idea how my students or the program could sustain such an expense.

I consulted with my director, Kari, and she agreed that we would take a leap of faith. Each family that could was asked to donate ten dollars for their child to make a scrapbook. No child would be turned away if unable to pay. I took registrations and went shopping. I was able to buy each child a glue stick and a small five-by-seven-inch spiral-bound scrapbook.

I decided that I would donate everything else, including stickers, stencils, paper, die cuts, letters and embellishments. The class was a hit! In fact, it grew to two classes a week that were one hour, but then became two-hour classes.

I decided to put out an SOS online for donations. I belonged to three Yahoo scrapbook groups, and I asked for donations of any kind for my after-school kids. Little did I know what big hearts scrapbookers have!

Boxes started to come in from all over the United States—Georgia, Illinois, New York, California, Mississippi, everywhere! We received scrapbooks, paper, idea books, scissors, adhesive, anything and everything you could ever want.

The children were so excited about each and every box and carefully looked at the treasures these strangers had packed for them with love. Everyone wrote thank-you notes to our special friends, and we soon became acquainted with the geography of the United States by looking up where our new friends lived.

The scrapbooking club evolved into an unplanned educational experience. Children learned math from measuring, using geometric shapes to make their layouts. Writing became an important art, as perfect spelling and handwriting were needed in journaling. Keen attention was paid to how colors complement each other and how to use pictures to tell a story.

Cooperative learning was evident at every class. Students shared their work up and down the halls of school. Members of the club found items for each other to enhance layouts and encouraged each other with praise and suggestions for improvement.

As a teacher I learned that every child and family have a story to share. I am so blessed to have online friends who cared and shared with an after-school scrapbook club in Cavalier, North Dakota.

Scrapbooking isn't about scraps of paper and photos. Scrapbooking is about scraps of life—yours and those special to you.

Cheryl Neumann

Memories in the Making

There is no distance too far between friends, for friendship gives wings to the heart.

Kathy Kay Benudiz

"T wo thousand miles," I muttered at the bunny bouncing across my computer screen. "Two thousand miles!" *Boing, boing, boing.* Another rabbit hopped into view. I heaved a huge sigh and pushed the "Send" button.

When our granddaughter was born three years ago, I'd rued the distance separating us—but now I resented it. No longer an infant, engaging little Avery was developing a memory, and I wanted to be certain we held a firm place in it.

Phone calls helped, but too often she shied away from conversation or nodded her silent answers. The periodic e-mails I forwarded entertained her momentarily—especially those featuring noises and animated graphics—yet there was no real lasting benefit. But Avery did love getting mail, her mother assured me, even though she couldn't read.

That's it! I grabbed a file folder full of memorabilia. *I'll send her mail that doesn't need to be read.*

Simple but brilliant, the concept would be inexpensive, creative and toddler-friendly: a traveling scrapbook. Already I'd documented all our visits to the East Coast and hers to Colorado by saving ticket stubs from the choo-choo ride, original "artwork" she'd crayoned, a ribbon she'd finally wrestled from our toy poodle's fresh coiffure . . . .

And pictures, lots and lots of pictures. Ever diligent, my husband, a professional photographer, had documented it all. Of her. Of us. Of all our memorable times together. Oh, we'd made memories all right, and they were good ones. But time and distance could easily steal them from our granddaughter.

So Pops and I set to work on Avery's Airborne Album.

We opted for a petite four-by-six-inch size, roomy enough to accommodate the photos with ample space on the left for punching two holes. We laminated each page, making it suitable for eager, incautious young fingers. And we snapped on binder rings—large enough to handle the additional pages we planned to mail over time—and slipped the diminutive portfolio into a padded envelope and sent it off.

"Avery, tell Grammy and Pops what came in the mail today," I heard my daughter prompt into the phone.

"My little book," Avery squealed, "My little book with choo-choo tickets and pictures."

"Pictures of what?" I asked.

"Of the conductor. 'All a-bo-ard,' he said 'All a-bo-ard!'"

"What else?" I encouraged, delighted at her sudden chattiness.

"At the park. *Be*-member? And Grammy and Avery making Easter cookies. *Be*-member?" Her tongue nearly tripped over her mounting excitement. "Cookies with sprinkles. *Be*-member, Grammy?"

"Oh, yes, sweetie," I grinned into the phone. "Of course, I remember." My voice lowered to a satisfied whisper. "And now, so do you!"

Carol McAdoo Rehme

The Christmas Not Missed

The more you praise and celebrate your life, the more there is in life to celebrate.

Oprah Winfrey

ecember is a difficult month to forget, especially this particular one in 2002. I spent most of the month not planning a Christmas, but rather watching a machine breathe for my father and praying for a Christmas miracle. Seven years ago previously, my mother had died, and now my dad was in a coma in the intensive care unit (ICU).

My family was gathered together, not around a Christmas tree, but around a hospital bed, and we were feeling quite blue. All of a sudden it struck me . . . my mother never permitted us to be sad at Christmastime, and since Dad lived at my house, he always made me put out the decorations, even the year Mom had died so unexpectedly. He told us, "If we don't honor Christmas, then our faith is in vain." Why should this year be any different? Shame on me for not following the family traditions—I was not making cookies, planning holiday dinners, wrapping the presents or even putting out the Nativity scene. So, home I went to get myself moving in full gear and fill our house with the holiday spirit.

I wanted everything to be like all the holidays before. And while I prepared for Christmas, Dad hung on. He never gave up. He came out of his coma and breathed on his own, but he did not know who he was, where he was or even that we were there. He knew he wanted coffee, so I stopped my baking long enough to bring him iced coffee chips.

Christmas came, and we celebrated the holiday as best we could under the circumstances. Then came New Year's, and my brother made the effort to watch college football with Dad, which he so loved. Sadly, Dad was not even aware that the television in his room was on, but we continued to nurture and be there for him anyway.

One exceptionally trying day, I asked his physician, "Is there any guarantee Dad will ever know us again?"

Sadly she replied, "There is no way of predicting such a thing."

It was as if Dad could hear our pleas. The next day, I walked in and he said, "Hi, Sher, how are you doing?" and beamed his big smile. I raced over and hugged him.

Dad continued to get stronger mentally and physically. Valentine's Day came; I cooked him his favorite meal, taking it to my "true love"—Dad—at the rehab center. He ate his fried oysters, honey slaw, baked sweet potato and coconut cake, and only complained because I brought "too much," but he ate every bite. While he was eating, I turned on the television. He watched me scrapbook with the cable anchor for fifteen minutes. He loved to watch me bring old pictures to life in my scrapbooking when we were home together. I am also a scrapbook teacher, and he'd help by retrieving supplies for me, knowing the scrapbooking "terms" better than most men. So I knew he would enjoy seeing me teach on television. Dad would call the nurses in from the hall, saying, "Look, my daughter's on TV!"

After it was over, he looked at me and said, "Did you scrapbook Christmas?"

I looked at him and said, "Do you mean this Christmas?" He nodded "yes" to me. Tears were in his eyes, and he said, "I missed it."

I jumped up, saying, "No! you didn't!" and I raced home for the pages.

He and I laughed that night about the cookies. I was now able to tell him how I had to stop baking because he wanted coffee and was only allowed ice chips, so I had to freeze them. It was all documented on the page of our cookies! And then there was the crooked tree and my journaling saying that Dad wasn't there to straighten it, but at least I got it up! And the presents—his were under the tree, and we opened them in January, covering him with his Phillies blanket and bringing him a decorated tree one of our neighbors brought for him.

He looked at each page and then asked, "Where's Christmas dinner?"

I laughed and said, "Look at the snow! We couldn't get to each other, so we had to wait until two days later!" As I watched him turn each page, he smiled more.

When we got to the Penn State bowl game, he frowned. I said, "Yes, you weren't there for the bowl game," but in his true wit, he said, "Neither was Penn State from what I hear." They had lost badly.

What a great time we had. I knew he hadn't missed Christmas; I had saved it for him! Dad had given me the best Christmas gift of all that year, his silent voice telling me not to skip the holiday, but to celebrate as always.

He slipped away to be with Mom the Friday after Father's Day, and I miss him so. But I now know the value of saving every moment of my life, as it's all so precious. Dad had put meaning into my scrapbooking hobby. I don't want anyone to forget what a special person he was, but now they won't because Dad taught me one of his most valuable lessons in the final months of his life. Celebrate always, for life is not to be missed.

Sharon Knopic

From the Heart, for Alex

The wisdom of love . . . the highest wisdom ever known upon this Earth.

Charles Dickens

As I was driving home from work one sunny afternoon, I began thinking about my oldest brother John who, at the age of thirty-two, had passed away a few short years ago after fighting a very courageous battle against cancer. I began thinking about John's wife, Janet, and their four children he left behind. Alex, the oldest of the four kids, was only nine years old when his daddy passed. I thought about how Alex, now almost eighteen, looks so much like his father. Alex is preparing to graduate high school soon, and I began to think of how proud my brother would have been of his son. I pictured John at Alex's graduation, beaming from ear to ear over his little boy who has now grown into a wonderful young man. I began to wish like crazy that my brother could be here to witness his son's graduation and share with him the wisdom that he used to share with us as younger siblings. I wondered how I could relay to Alex how proud his daddy would have been and also share with Alex some words of wisdom his daddy may have passed on to him as this chapter of his life closes and he opens a new chapter.

I will never forget that moment, as I was driving in my car with all of these emotions whirling around in me, when the idea struck. All of these thoughts led me to the conclusion that I could use my passion for scrapbooking to relay these precious thoughts and feelings to my nephew. What a perfect way for all of our family to contribute to his graduation. Through pictures and journaling, we could all share thoughts and feelings about my brother that are sometimes too difficult to speak about. We could use this medium to share things that sometimes the whirlwind of life passes by. Alex, in turn, could reflect on these thoughts and feelings about his father in his own time and at his leisure—whether in private thought or together with his mother and siblings.

After speaking with Janet and my family about the idea, my project of sharing my brother's life, thoughts, dreams and wishes commenced. I put together a questionnaire for those closest to John, including Janet, my parents, my siblings, my aunt and uncle, and my grandmother. The questionnaire covered items I thought Alex and his siblings would enjoy knowing. Questions like, what is your funniest memory of John? Which of John's personality traits did you admire the most? Describe John as a son/brother/husband, and finally, what advice do you think John would like to share with Alex upon his graduation? The response I received was amazing. The time, thoughts and emotions that were put into this effort were truly a tribute to my oldest brother. I had plenty of written material for our scrapbook—now to hunt for photos. Janet graciously offered a photo album that she had put together, and I raided my mother's photo boxes for others.

It is now March, and Alex graduates this May. I am beginning to assemble all of this wonderful material into what I hope will be a very memorable gift from the hearts of many for Alex—a gift beyond money and gift certificates, a gift that will last a lifetime. I pray that I can adequately piece together an album that will speak from my brother, through us, to his oldest son at such a memorable time in his life. I am so thankful for this wonderful hobby of scrapbooking that allows me to share with Alex some very dear and precious thoughts and feelings that might otherwise be difficult to share.

Karen Helsen

The One I Never Forgot

I love thee with the breath,
smiles and tears of all my life . . .

Elizabeth Barrett Browning

I've been a scrapbooker for years, and it's one of my life's true passions. But it came to a screeching halt when my marriage ended after seventeen years. I looked at all my scrapbooks of our life together and thought it was all just wasted. I felt I had been scrapbooking a lie; I thought I would never be able to scrapbook again.

I really struggled to get through each day, and the pain seemed to be endless. I prayed constantly for God to help me and to restore my marriage. I was unable to do even the simplest things and had no interest in the things that had given me joy in the past. My friends, however, wouldn't let me give up. They encouraged me to get back to my favorite activities and hobbies, so little by little over the next year, I gradually started trying to scrapbook again. First, I did a small album of the animals I've loved in my life. That wasn't too bad. So I tried my heritage book, but somehow I couldn't get into it and finally just gave up.

One year after my world had fallen apart, I was still praying for a miracle, and it seemed my prayers were going unheard. I didn't understand why God was letting me suffer so. But I refused to give up. I celebrated with my friends that I had survived such a traumatic, painful year. And I made a promise to myself that I would reclaim my life, and I would no longer let my husband's poor choices consume the rest of my life. I began to feel that God had something planned for me. That whole year I'd had a Scripture taped to my mirror from Jeremiah 29:11, *"I know the plans I have for you, plans for your welfare and not for calamity, to give you a future and a hope."* After a year of reading this daily, I finally began to actually believe in this promise.

So I looked for something I could enjoy, and I decided to return to my passion for scrapbooking. My father had died when I was eight years old, and my mother and I moved to a small town nearby where we had some family. I had started third grade in a new school and made new friends. I thought this might be a good place to start scrapbooking again.

One of those childhood friends was a boy named Mike. We sat next to each other at school, and I thought he was just so cute, funny and smart. He and I lived a block apart, went to school together every day and did our homework together every night. We also went to every church service together since Mike's parents were in the choir and my mother was the organist. We were very close; we had a connection and a bond that lasted, though we never dated. I was so crazy about Mike, but he apparently never realized how I felt about him. We subsequently married others, but we never completely lost touch. Every time we

saw each other, we knew that connection was still there, but we were
committed to others.

Starting to scrapbook with my
third-grade photos was a good
choice because I had such
fond memories of those days.
My mother, a true pack rat,
had kept everything, so I
had valentines from Mike,
notes we wrote to each other in church and even something I had written up about him when I was thirteen. The
valentines Mike had given me said, "I love you" and "I love
you more than 'eny' in the world" and many more such
sentiments. As I scrapbooked these memories, I reflected
on those days with Mike so long ago.

Several months passed, and our high school had a class
reunion. I had finished my scrapbooks all the way through
high-school graduation by then; my classmates pored over
them at the reunion, laughing, reminiscing and telling
stories. Mike wasn't interested in attending the reunion,
but two of our closest friends urged him to meet the three
of us for breakfast the next day. I didn't know if Mike
would come or not, but I was really hoping he would. Both
of us were divorced by then, but I had no expectations
other than just visiting with a guy I had so many good
memories with.

The morning we were to meet for breakfast, no one
knew for sure if Mike was coming or not. Suddenly, there
he was, and my heart skipped a beat. I felt thirteen again.
The four of us enjoyed a leisurely breakfast together. As
the others headed back to their respective homes about
noon, Mike asked me to stay and visit with him for a

while; neither of us was eager to leave. We talked nonstop for hours and on into the evening. He wanted to see the scrapbooks, and I was embarrassed to show him the things I had kept as well as the things I had written about him when I was young. He wasn't embarrassed at all; in fact, he was flattered, and the scrapbooks brought back many wonderful memories for us.

Mike told me later that he had felt a small, but insistent voice telling him to go to that breakfast, and when he walked in and saw me, he knew why he had gone. Something happened that day, and God blessed us abun-dantly. We believe it was God's timing for this meeting, and God's plans were finally becoming clear. Mike and I had both been through some very painful times, and both of us had been afraid to trust again. But when we saw each other, we knew "here was someone we could trust." God did the rest, and he opened our hearts and blessed us with love.

We married a few months later, surrounded by our families and friends. At the wedding, we displayed the scrapbook pages with both our mementos, which traced our history from third grade on, including those valentines, notes, photos and stories. Our wedding guests pored over them with amazement and joy. These pages are now the introductory pages to our wedding scrapbook.

Now we really do love each other "more than 'eny' in the world." I have a new life to capture in my scrapbooks and the love of the one I never forgot.

Mary Mason

I Promise

Illness is a convent which has its rule, its austerity, its silences and its inspirations.

Albert Camus

It was early April, on a warm, overcast Easter morning, when I asked my parents if they would like to go out and sit on their wooden porch swing that my mother loved so much. My three children had already scouted out all of the hidden Easter eggs and consumed most of the sugary candy that the Easter Bunny had left for them in brightly colored baskets tied with funky bows. After stuffing themselves endlessly, they retreated to my parents' front yard to frolic and play in the warm breeze while the rest of us watched. My father was very sick, and I knew that he would not see another Easter as his cancer had mercilessly spread throughout his body, so I led him to the porch swing with my mother close behind. Seeing the two of them sit together on that red cedar swing quickly proved to be one of my fondest memories, for it was at that time that I realized how important the little things are in life.

As they sat, conversing about everything from the laughter of their grandchildren to my father's wishes for his funeral, I pulled out my camera and quietly snapped many, many pictures of the two of them as they shared close conversation with each other. I photographed my mom's hand on my father's frail shoulder, completely fascinated by how a woman who was faced with spending the rest of her life alone could be so stoic and brave in the face of her impending loneliness, which would come all too soon. I zoomed in on the tiny lines of my father's face, wondering what he was thinking as they continued to swing together, watching their grandchildren play in the green grass. Suddenly, while taking photograph after photograph, a somewhat empty feeling washed over me as I realized that I had wasted too much precious time over the years, not capturing the everyday memories that would carry us through once our loved ones were gone. I had relied strictly on my memory to contain all of the important events as time sped by. My mind raced with many simple yet meaningful events that had previously escaped me and the range of my camera, only to hope that the memories of those past events could remain forever etched in my brain. I began to wish for the clock to rewind so that I could go back and take pictures of all the everyday pieces of life that made us who we are.

Sure, I had photographs of Christmases past, birthday parties and graduation ceremonies that we had attended as a family, but I had very few pictures of my parents enjoying the simple things in life that ultimately made them who they are as individuals. I had no photos of my dad tending to his beloved grapevines that he carefully planted each year. I had no photos of my mother watching television or quietly putting together jigsaw puzzles with many pieces, as she so often did to forget her worries.

These everyday moments had escaped me over the years, disappearing right in front of my very own eyes, and it was too late to save them on film for my children to see as I once had. At that moment, I snapped even more photos of my parents together on that porch swing, faster and more furiously than ever, in an effort to try to freeze some of my dad's final days with all of us. I see strength and devotion in those pictures of my parents, and I see that true love transcends all things, even in the face of difficulty.

On that day, I learned one of the most valuable lessons I have ever learned in my twenty-nine years of life, and that is to capture each moment for future generations to cherish, for once we die, those memories that are permanently etched in our minds also die with us. We cannot share those mental pictures once we are gone; we must take the time to visually document the simple things that make each of us who we are. I vowed at that moment to spend more quality time learning about what makes my family so unique, and to take the time to notice and record the little things that we never want to forget about those who are dear to us.

My father passed away a little over a month later, and I am so thankful for those photos that I took of him before he died. Those who knew him well did not like to see those painful photos of him toward the end, as they could easily see how quickly his health deteriorated, but my children and I have found great comfort in those final close-up photographs, as they captured his strong will to live despite the intransigent cancer that slowly overcame him. I have created scrapbook pages to reflect my feelings about my dad so that my children will always remember some of the very things that I remember about him. He zestfully lived for each day and believed that we should all do the same. Thank you, Dad, for your valuable lesson; I promise to do just that.

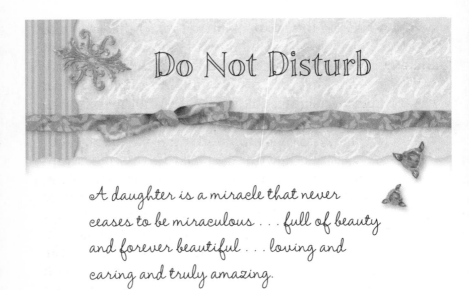

Do Not Disturb

*A daughter is a miracle that never
ceases to be miraculous . . . full of beauty
and forever beautiful . . . loving and
caring and truly amazing.*

Deanna Beisser

have always been a crafty person: sewing, painting, crocheting, scrapbooking, writing, stamping—you name it, I've done it. I had been published several times in the past, but it just got to be too much. I was no longer doing arts and crafts on a whim with no boundaries and to please myself—I was doing them to please the style of a magazine or publishing company. So I stopped submitting my artwork and crafts. A sigh of relief came when I was able to make something special for a friend or family member without having to say, "Oh, yeah . . . I might need that back for a while to send to a magazine editor if they decide they want to publish my idea." And keeping track of every tiny little detail of what manufacturer made what and where this or that can be bought was no longer necessary. And you really have to have excellent technical writing skills for the "how-to" write-up, so that pressure was gone. It took the wisdom of a seven-year-old to put things in perspective when I started to fall back into my old habits—crafting for praise, profit and publishers and not for personal enjoyment. There's just nothing like the voice of reason when it comes from the mouth of a child.

When I got back into scrapbooking this past year, I suddenly found myself captivated by a Web site where scrappers shared downloaded images of their layouts along with the techniques and products they used to create them. Each evening after work, dinner, chores and helping my daughter with her homework, I would squeeze in an hour or two of scrapbooking. I would sit in front of the computer, my desk covered in scrapping supplies, with my favorite scrapping Web site up on the screen. More often than not, most of my time would be spent collecting ideas from other scrappers. Some layouts are very intricate, detailed and expensive. Some are just simple layouts with minimal fuss and products. I started out doing the simple layouts—a few matted photos per page with an element or two, like stickers. Little by little, the addiction grew. I wanted to be one of those people who posted ideas daily, got dozens of compliments, participated in contests and was always up-to-date with the new products. I wanted to start submitting my artistic wares to publishers again.

My seven-year-old daughter, Baileigh, is also an avid scrapbooker. We share supplies, ideas and paper, and we are each other's biggest fans when it comes to critiquing our layouts. Baileigh has no limitations when it comes to her scrapbooking. She does her scrapbooking layouts for herself and no one else, and she doesn't care if anyone likes them or not. She says, "They are my pictures, my memories and my style. I'm not being graded." One day, she saw that I was getting a little cranky while scrapbooking a single layout for over two hours. She said to me, "Mommy, why don't you just take a break from your layout and play with me? I am pretending to teach a class on scrapbooking." Baileigh was always pretending to do something; after all, she's little. I told her that I was sorry, but I just had to finish what I was doing and I would play later.

The next day, I was doing the same thing—working on a layout, typing up the instructions, stressing out as usual. She again asked me, "Mommy, take a break and come scrap with me. I'm doing a special page today." Again, I declined her invite. A couple days later, I was creating a set of handmade cards for an online auction, and my daughter was scrapbooking by herself. She was very quiet other than the soft humming she was doing while gluing, cutting and cropping away on a layout. She asked me a couple of times how to spell some words that she wasn't sure about, but when she asked me how to spell "disturb," I was a little curious about what she was doing. I asked her, "Honey, what are you making?" She looked up at me, smiling from ear to ear, and held up her nearly finished layout. My heart sank, and my eyes welled up with tears. She had created a layout with about six pictures of me sitting at my desk working diligently on my designs, and the title read, "Do Not Disturb! Busy Mom at Work!"

I looked at the pictures, mostly of the back of my head, and realized I had never even seen them before. Baileigh had been taking pictures with her throwaway camera for weeks. I had them developed and gave them to her, but I had never even looked at them. Her journaling was on a neat little tag she made herself and it read, "My mom is great. She works hard on her layouts, and people buy them and copy her. She is too busy to play because she cares what people think. I think everything she does is great!" The tears wouldn't stay for long, and a couple ran down my cheeks. Baileigh asked me, "Why are you crying? Don't you like it?" Her smile disappeared. I hit the off button of my computer, not saving a single thing first, grabbed everything off my desk in one short motion and put everything away. I went over to her and hugged her with every ounce of my being.

"Wow! You must like it a lot! It made you cry and hug me," she said. I smiled, wiped the mascara-tinted tears from my face and said, "It's the most beautiful piece of artwork I have ever seen. And it made me realize something." Baileigh gave me a puzzled look and asked what I was talking about. I explained to her, "Your layout made me realize that the back of my head is boring. You should see the front of my head much more than you already do when I am scrapbooking." So I sat down on the floor with Baileigh, surrounded by all of her art supplies, and we scrapped three pages in a row. They were all about mothers and daughters doing stuff together and had several fun pictures of the two of us together. On one layout Baileigh handwrote the words, "Who cares what other people think . . . Just create happiness for yourself!"

I stopped spending hours every night scrapping in my own little world and by everyone else's standards. I now scrap for me. If I like it, then that's what matters. I have created happiness for myself . . . and for the little ones around me.

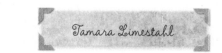

Tamara Limestahl

Memories

Anyone can be a father, but it takes someone special to be a daddy.

Author Unknown

N o, Mom, I'm not going. I mean it." The unthinkable had happened. My father had gone to the doctor's office for a heart catheter and had been admitted for quadruple bypass surgery. I had no idea what that was, but I could see by the fear on my mother's usually strong face that it was bad, even dangerous. And here I was, scheduled to leave on one of my favorite annual summer camps, two hours away. I was not, however, leaving my daddy. He needed his little girl.

"Honey, you should go. It'll distract you."

"I don't want to be distracted. I'm needed here right now. Daddy needs me. You need me."

"Honey, you need to go."

My mother did get her way at last, and as we all loaded our luggage on the buses and had our last pizza party before heading off, the story quietly circulated. My closest friends knew that my rising and setting sun was my father.

Their parents, most of whom knew my parents, said they were sorry and told me stories about my dad. When I got to camp, I couldn't concentrate on anything. During free time, I stayed in my cabin, staring at a picture of my father and me at my junior prom. Not having a date, I took my father. It was the best prom I ever had.

Suddenly, I had an idea. I went to the camp phone (which I had unlimited access to because of the circumstances) and called not my mother, but my best friend. His parents and my parents had been friends as long as I could remember. I talked to my best friend's mom and asked her if she could remember any funny stories of my dad. Oh, boy, could she! My dad's a funny guy, so I bet it wasn't that hard. We talked for hours. When I got off the phone, I looked at the notes I had taken and raced back to my cabin. For the next four days, I spent all my free time in my cabin, writing out these stories and ones I knew as well—incidences, memories, a scrapbook of words featuring a picture of my father in front, a lifetime of memories behind. When I left my cabin the last day of camp, I was more ready than ever to be home, but I was smiling. These stories made me less lonely for Daddy. During the evening sermon, a woman came running down the aisle and handed a slip to the pastor, who stopped midsermon.

"Is there an Alonnya Schemer here?" he asked.

I raised my hand shakily. I knew that slip. It was a phone message. No one would have called unless it was urgent.

"Daddy?"

"There is a phone message from your mother here. It says your father has been released from the hospital and will be home to see you tomorrow."

The entire assembly erupted in cheers, and I was smothered in a many-armed hug as people cried out congratulations and happiness. When I got home, I waited for Daddy. When I saw him, he was sitting down in his chair. Except for his mussed hair, he looked like he always did. Still, the road to recovery was hard and long. I was there every step of the way, and I told my dad about the stories I had written. When he was truly well, we looked at the stories and laughed together at some of the funny things I remembered. That was when my father asked me to write his biography, and he told me more stories. He had done so many things! I began the biography, titling it, "The Man with Many Faces." He has done many different things, but the best thing of all is being a daddy. The pages of Daddy's Scrapbook prove that.

Alonnya Schemer

I Thanked Her for It Later

Let us be grateful to people who make us happy; they are the charming gardeners who make our souls blossom.

Marcel Proust

In my eyes, my mom is "Superwoman!" She has talent beyond compare and is always capturing the lives of my sisters and me in one way or another. As wonderful as my mom is, I am not like her. But the one thing we do share in common is our contempt for clichés—they irritate us. Even so, there has been one phrase that has been repeated many, many times during my childhood. As Mom followed us, camera in hand, from every tennis match, to soccer game, to Bat Mitzvah lesson, to prom hair appointment—making us promise to save any ticket stub, show program, matchbook or memento that we came across—my two younger sisters and I were victim to the old, "You'll thank me for this later." As we planned our family vacations, and the driving routes were mapped out around scrapbook stores, she always reminded us that we would "be grateful later on." And when she made me hang back from the rest of the group during my first college tour so she could take a picture of me in front of the university's big iron gates, she promised me that "one day" I would thank her for it.

To be honest, I never believed her. I mean, scrapbooking made my mom happy, and when she was happy, she tended to spend more time in her scrapbook room and less time telling me to get off-line and clean out my closet—and for this I was always grateful. Mom's scrapbooks were always fun to look at. My friends especially liked to take my high-school album off the shelf and find themselves in the many pages that my mom had labored over. My sisters loved to look at the pages of their birthday parties, dance recitals and basketball games. I loved any page where my hair looked all right and my braces weren't on. I enjoyed my mom's books, of course, and I recognized her talent for scrapbooking, as well as for photography, but I don't know that I was ever overcome with gratitude.

Along with just about every other aspect of my life, this changed the day I was accepted to my first-choice college. I realized then that of all the important things that will happen in my life after my high-school graduation, there will not be many more that I will be home to experience. Beyond that, even the little things my mom scrapbooked— from random days at school, to football games, to the series finale of *Friends* that made me cry—would not mean as much to anyone else in the world as they did to her.

I am so grateful that my mom has spent the time, money, talent and energy to record and celebrate every

moment of my first seventeen years. I
am grateful for the physical aspect of
the books: the beauty of the papers,
stamps and letters that she used. I
am grateful for the gift I have been
given of memories: These books are a yearbook
of my life, with all the people and things I love,
highlighted with emphasis on all of the significant
moments. She gets such enormous joy from making sure
my sisters and I are aware of the fact that every little
thing we do means the world to her. I have never felt
more loved or important than the day I realized the one
thing in the world that makes my mom happiest is when
she is spending time on my life: taking pictures, writing
about it, finding papers that embody it and making note
of its every minute.

Arielle Napp

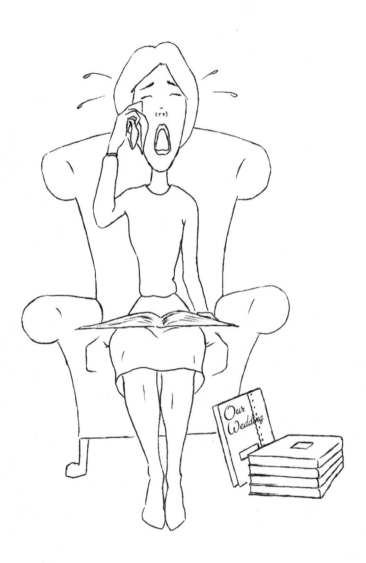

Reprinted by permission of Mack Dobbie ©2005.

The Little Black Scrapbook

*Every gift from a friend is
a wish for your happiness.*

Richard Bach

"**S**crapbooking—what a complete and total crazy maker! Piles and piles of albums with overly decorated pages, a whole closet in your home for all the papers, tools, gee-gaws and books connected with it. Throw the photos into Rubbermaid containers labeled by topic and forget about them!"

This was the long-held opinion of my dearest friend Julie. Julie is a minimalist. In spite of that, she's my closest friend and soul sister. Friends forgive each other their faults and eccentricities, right?

Julie tolerated my camera as it was toted along on our hikes, shopping outings and other shared activities. She celebrated with me when my first layout publication appeared, and well she should have. The layout featured the both of us getting a second piercing in our ears.

Still, if conversation over coffee or long walks turned toward my obsession, invariably Julie would say something like, "Gwyn, you know I love ya, but this is just NUTS! Will either of your boys appreciate needing to hire a forklift to haul out all these photo albums when you're gone? It's a burden, not a gift!" Sometimes, she almost had me convinced . . . almost.

Her son Greg would be graduating from high school soon, and in my long hours sitting around their house, I'd enjoyed conversations with him. I'd seen him grow from an awkward nine-year-old when they first moved here to this intelligent young man ready to move into adulthood. From what Julie had told me, Greg actually enjoyed our conversations, too, and wasn't just being polite. Instead of the usual Target gift certificates we'd given many graduating seniors, I felt like I had more history with him than that. What better way than to make a small gift scrapbook?

I didn't want to ask for photos to fill the pages, ruining the surprise element of this gift. Instead I went through pictures I'd taken over the years and developed my theme around the incidents I saw as part of shaping who he had become.

I had so much fun pulling this together from bits and pieces and, storyteller that I am, weaving together seemingly disparate events into a cohesive story of Greg. It wasn't "publication worthy," but that wasn't the point.

Graduation came and went. We stopped at Greg's home on our circuit of open houses that day. My gift was left on the gift table and our congratulations were shared.

After a few days, curiosity took over. I asked Julie what he thought. She didn't know.

"Why on earth not? Didn't he open it? Did you see it?

What did you think?" Attempts to play it cool were failing utterly.

Julie told me they had yet to actually see what it was. Oh, they'd seen the little black album, so she knew it was some sort of scrapbook. She just hadn't seen beyond the cover.

I felt my heart sink. I'd really blown it. What in the world was I thinking that an eighteen-year-old boy would want such a thing? This scrapbooking stuff really had made me crazy—crazy enough to ever think this was an appropriate gift for him.

About a week later, Julie and I were doing what teachers with the summer off will do—bumming on the deck. She had invited me over for lunch. As we settled into place with our iced teas, I could see she was brimming with something exciting to tell me.

"Gwyn, I totally get it now!"

"Get what?" I had no idea what on earth she meant.

"Your scrapbooks. Greg finally let us see the one you made him. It's his favorite of all the graduation gifts he received."

Apparently, he had kept it for himself when he first viewed it, not wanting to share it right away, even with his parents. She said he'd study it and read it over and over. When he finally let the rest of the family see it, he said he couldn't believe how well I knew him. He wondered if I'd been writing all these little stories down over the past ten years. He said that it was the only gift he received from anyone that showed any thought about who he was as a person.

Julie finally understood that this "crazy scrapbooking" could be a gift, not a burden. The words woven with images on those few pages told a story of her son with humor and compassion. Now she actually asked to see other pages I'd done and enjoyed seeing the story of our friendship displayed across those layouts.

When Greg packed up to leave for Stanford a few months later, they sorted through all the things he would need to take with him. Like his mother, Greg is a minimalist. There wasn't much he needed to take or keep—his keyboard, his guitar, some books, clean underwear and socks. He did not bring the little black scrapbook.

The little black scrapbook needed to stay with his parents, he said, where it would be safe during his college years, with specific instructions that if the house were to start on fire, it would be the first thing to grab on the way out. This was the ultimate testament to the value of my work, from an eighteen-year-old boy and his mom . . . who now "gets it."

Gwyn Calvetti

Two Peas in a Pod

Love is composed of a single soul inhabiting two bodies.

Aristotle

From the moment Curtis and I met in the summer of 2001, he asserted that I am his inspiration for writing poetry. Early on in our relationship, my handsome husband made a promise to write poems for me as often as he could, but most definitely on the days he doesn't get to kiss my lips. And I made a promise to Curtis that I would scrapbook all of his poems so our posterity can have an everlasting memory of our journey through life.

In November 2003, we discovered that both of our promises would surely be put to the test. Two days after Thanksgiving, Curtis and I returned home from a weekend getaway at his parents' condo in the mountains. As we pressed the button to listen to our messages on the answering machine, we had no idea the extent to which our lives were about to change as the result of one simple message. "This is so and so with the National Guard . . ." was all Curtis needed to hear to almost faint with fear, knowing that the news was not good. He knew that something big was on the horizon. As Curtis returned the gentleman's call, the next few minutes seemed to last forever as we waited to find out the reason for the call. Curtis's National Guard unit was being deployed.

The news was devastating. My heart sank. So many questions inundated my mind. How long will he be gone? Will he be deployed to Iraq? When would he be leaving? Nothing can prepare you for news like this. It is heart-breaking to hear that your loved one will be in harm's way, but at the same time, you feel admiration knowing that your soldier is willing to defend freedom. Not a lot of details about the deployment were available at the time so, naturally, we had a lot of questions and no answers. It wasn't until a short time later we found out that Curtis was going to Afghanistan for up to eighteen months.

The first week of January 2004, Curtis and I sat on a duffel bag, eating Peanut Butter M&Ms, in an airport hangar, knowing that the inevitable was about to happen. My husband, my soldier, would have to board the bus and travel to his first destination, Colorado, in which he would go through several months of training. After Curtis and the rest of the soldiers lined up for roll call, Curtis and I walked hand in hand outside to the buses. I didn't want to let him go, but I knew I had to. I watched Curtis get on the bus and then stood there for a while smiling at him and blowing kisses in the frigid air. I didn't care about the cold weather. I didn't want to leave. Unfortunately, the buses eventually drove away, and the only thing left for me to do was walk back to the car.

Before arriving at the hangar, I told myself to stay strong for Curtis and keep my emotions intact. After all, there was nothing he could do to change the situation. I wanted to be strong for Curtis and not make the situation any harder for him, so I held in my tears until I got back to the car. Then the floodgates opened, and I let it go. Watching the buses drive off into the distance was bittersweet—bitter because my handsome husband had just left, and sweet because it meant that I would be getting something very special every day of the deployment. The special something is a poem. Curtis desired to keep his promise by writing a poem each day that we are apart during his deployment.

Over four hundred poems later, Curtis still hasn't stopped writing them, and he will continue to write one each day until the very end of this separation when he can once again kiss my lips. I love the fact that the other soldiers recognize Curtis as "the guy who writes his wife a poem every day." For the past year, I've looked forward to getting a phone call each night from my handsome husband. Hearing his voice and listening to him read the poem that he wrote for me that day is very comforting. It gives me joy, strength and peace of mind.

That joy continues as I keep my promise to scrapbook all of Curtis's poems. When I first started scrapping, I never imagined I would be using the talent to create a memory book of hundreds of poems. Curtis and I are "two peas in a pod." He writes the poems, and I scrapbook them. It is an honor to support my handsome husband in his deployment and scrapbook the poems he writes for me. It will be an honor for me to one day tell our children about Curtis's service to our country and share his legacy of poems, and it will be captured not only in my heart, but in my scrapbook as well.

Mindy Barrow

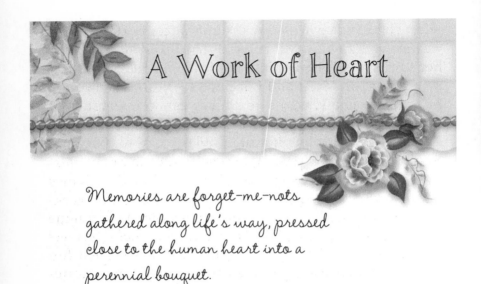

A Work of Heart

Memories are forget-me-nots gathered along life's way, pressed close to the human heart into a perennial bouquet.

Clara Smith Reber

One of the most valuable lessons my mother taught me is the importance of always having film in my camera. We lived a simple life, and there were not a lot of extras when my sister, brother and I were growing up. However, there was always an abundance of love and never a shortage of photographs. Our parents had a gift for capturing the candid moment. During all the school programs, one of them would have the aisle seat with camera in hand . . . usually Daddy because Mom had a tendency to chop off heads. Many hours have been spent poring over the photograph books that Mom kept; she was scrapbooking long before it became trendy.

Our parents had shared a very special relationship. I sometimes believed that one of them inhaled and the other exhaled. When Daddy died of cancer in 1996, a light was extinguished in Mom. We all tried so hard to bolster her spirits and keep her involved in life. With that as our inspiration, my sister and I decided to create a scrapbook for Mom to showcase those many years of memories. It would be a Christmas present.

Because we live one hundred miles apart, we began in July so we would have ample time to do the project justice. Since our time together always included activities with Mom, we had to safeguard our secret working weekends, hoping neither of us would have a slip of the tongue when talking to Mom. What wonderful memories we relived as we assembled our gift! We had so much fun pirating photos to copy and return without Mom's awareness. We laughed at some of the ridiculous stories we would concoct as excuses to dig through her stash. Mom told my sister after one of my visits, "Joan said she wanted pictures of herself as a teenager, but she kept getting in the wrong book." God bless Mom's trusting nature!

We chose a twelve-by-twelve-inch scrapbook in Mom's favorite color—a beautiful cranberry red—with "Memories" inscribed on the front cover. Our title page was her full name and the many roles she had throughout life (daughter, sister, wife, mother, friend, etc.) crossword-style. We started with pictures of her grandparents and parents. We then included baby pictures of Mom and historical information from the year she was born. It progressed with pictures of her family and friends, and then took a special turn when Daddy entered her life.

We had several photos of our parents when they were dating and, of course, their wedding photos—they had eloped on a weekend pass during World War II. We made a quick trip to a small town in Kansas to photograph, in black and white, the courthouse where they were married. They had only three short months together before he shipped out to Europe, but those three months were well documented with snapshots. We were even able to include a copy of the telegram he sent telling her he was coming home.

The scrapbook then highlighted our immediate family—pictures of my sister, brother and me as infants—followed by a lifetime of Christmases, anniversaries and, finally, a double-page layout of casual photos of Mom and Daddy together throughout their fifty-three years of marriage. Two of our favorite photos were taken at exactly the same location near Fort Lewis, Washington, over fifty years apart. The lyrics of Vince Gill's "Look at Us" edged the pages.

To appeal to Mom's sense of humor, we included a couple of fun pages of "Mom's Phobias & Favorites" and couldn't resist doing a tongue-in-cheek page of her "grand-dogs." As children, we were never allowed to have indoor pets, and she thought we had all slipped a cog by having house dogs. "Never underestimate the warmth of a cold nose."

Our plans for the remainder of the book were simple. My sister, brother and I would each provide a double-page layout with photos and personal memories of Mom. Each grandchild was assigned a single page and was given the same-sized journaling block to fill with his or her favorite memory of Grandma. Each great-grandchild would provide age-appropriate artwork.

How could we have possibly imagined she would never see it? In mid-October, Mom quietly and most unexpectedly passed away in her sleep. Rather than having the wonderful tribute to her life under the Christmas tree, it sat upon a stand for friends and family to view at her memorial, many pages still blank. Only one grandson had written his personal memory of Grandma, and it was included in her funeral service.

That was over two years ago. My sister and I have yet to complete the scrapbook, but we will . . . for the same reason it was begun . . . to honor her.

Joan Thezan

The Regifted Scrapbook

You don't choose your family. They are God's gift to you, as you are to them.

Desmond Tutu

I really couldn't get over how becoming a grandfather delighted my dad. I'll never forget how he looked as he rushed into my hospital room upon the arrival of his first grandson. The always neatly dressed, strict career military man that I was expecting showed up in full grandpa gear from head to toe. He was hilarious walking into the hospital in his "New Grandpa" hat and "When Mom says no, ask Grandpa" shirt with the bouquet of "It's a Boy" balloons. That crazy outfit started the hundreds of Grandpa pictures that I collected over the years. The next boy was actually named after him, which took things to a whole new level of Grandpa-mania. Bouncing a boy on each knee proved to be his life's greatest joy until . . . grandchild number three was a girl! The two dozen roses arrived at the hospital with notes to both of us. Mine read,

"May your daughter be the blessing to your life that you have been to mine!" and hers said, "Your very first roses from your very first sweetheart—Love, Grandpa."

He lived in Atlanta, about eight hours from us, and he always planned to travel the world during his retirement, but he decided that exotic destinations could wait, and he focused on family vacations that would give him more time with his only grandchildren. He called me constantly with very short notice and tickets to Disney World, Six Flags, Busch Gardens, Sea World, Williamsburg, Tweetsie Railroad—the list of fun vacation spots went on and on— all expenses paid by Grandpa. They were fabulous vacations, and he was always there with the camera in his hand. He loved the vacations, he loved the kids, and he loved taking pictures of it all.

After each vacation, he sent me several packs of pictures. I kept them all in a box until his sixty-fifth birthday came around. He was having a huge celebration, and I decided the best gift I could give would be a scrapbook of all the wonderful vacations we had taken. I had enough pictures to fill the entire scrapbook, which I appropriately entitled "Trippin' with Grandpa Ken." As I expected, he loved the book.

It was just a few months later when I got the call. He had passed out, and he was in the hospital. The news got worse with each update I received. It was a brain tumor, and it was malignant. I flew down for the surgery, which I was confident would solve the problem, but the day turned dark when the doctor reported that the cancer was terminal and, with intensive chemotherapy, he would be lucky to have a year left. Unwilling to accept the diagnosis, I remained in the denial stage. I just knew he would beat it. I just knew the chemo would do the trick, and I just knew

they'd find the cure for cancer long
before his time was up. It just wasn't
going to happen, and although I called
him every single day, I refused to ever
discuss the possibility that it would.
That was a big mistake and my
biggest regret.

The cancer spread much more
quickly than they anticipated, and
although doctors had given us a year, the final call came
just four months later. I went straight to the airport with
no suitcase, praying I'd make it in time to spend one more
moment with him. I was holding his hand when he died.

The next few days were a blur. I was helping to pick out
caskets, order flowers, and contact family and friends. The
happy pictures I held in my heart were replaced with new
images that were forever burned in my memory—my
father back in his military uniform, the twenty-one-gun
salute, and his beloved grandchildren holding each other as
they slowly walked forward and placed roses on his casket.

As I packed up to leave, I took the box of my father's
things that he had wanted me to have. I noticed that the
scrapbook was in there, but I didn't want to open it. It was
simply too painful. I knew it would only remind me of all
we would never share again—all that was now missing.

There were things I should have said, things I should
have let him say, but I deprived him, and I couldn't forgive
myself for that. Finally, right before what would have
been his sixty-sixth birthday, I opened the scrapbook, but
it didn't look like I remembered.

I was the mother of three young children, so although I
had taken the time to add all the pictures, there was
simply no time for journaling. The dedication was one of

the only things I had written, "Dedicated to Grandpa Ken with love. Thanks for everything."

Now underneath it read, "Rededicated to my daughter, who has brought me more joy in my lifetime than she could ever know. Thanks for this cherished book and for all the wonderful memories."

As I flipped through the pages I was expecting to recognize, I couldn't believe my eyes. They were all different. There were words on every page. There were envelopes and all sorts of surprises added in. Page by page, I flipped, and page by page, I was amazed at what the revised scrapbook contained.

On the Six Flags page, he had written about how my daughter had fallen and scraped her knee. He wrote that as he dried her tears, he carried her over to the ice-cream stand, and by the time she finished eating the cone, the pain had gone away. The attached envelope read, "It always worked on you, too, Suzy. I'm confident there's pain headed your way, but don't overlook the power of ice cream. It really does help."

I remembered when I was upset over little girl things, he used to take to me Baskin-Robbins and say, "They have thirty-one flavors here, so it's your mission to find at least one that can make you smile." I opened the envelope, and it was full of gift certificates for Baskin-Robbins.

There was a page from Tweetsie Railroad that featured a picture of him with the boys in a teepee. Attached were ten folded pieces of paper. The outside of each piece was dated and read, "For boys' eyes only!!"

He documented that the teepee was deemed "The Boys' Club," and while they were inside, they each had to tell one big secret, and they agreed to make the meetings an annual event. Those folded papers were his entries for the next ten years of Boys' Club meetings.

There were so many pictures and so many memories— lots of things I didn't even know about the trips. Among them was a picture of me riding hobbyhorses with the kids, and he had written, "You have given me so many reasons to be proud of you through the years: your grades, your grace, your numerous accomplishments, your kind and loving soul, and your limitless talents, but as I looked at you on the carousel, juggling all three kids on horses, laughing and leaning to kiss each one, smiling and waving at me, I have never been so proud. You are a wonderful mother, and your children are so lucky. Remember that as much as you love them and want to keep them on those horses, you are my child, and I want to keep you on your horse! Keep smiling and laughing and be happy no matter what. Life may not always turn out the way we'd like, but try to remember what you have instead of what you think you've lost."

When I finished reading all of his words, I knew he understood. I realized that he did know what I was feeling after all. On those pages he wrote what he felt, what he feared, and what he wanted from me after he was gone. It was unbelievable what the regifted scrapbook said to me. I laughed and I cried, and then I grabbed some of the Baskin-Robbins gift certificates and took my kids out for ice cream. They now have over fifty flavors, and we were on a mission.

Suzanne Walker

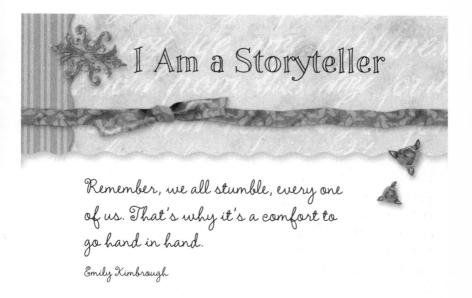

I Am a Storyteller

Remember, we all stumble, every one of us. That's why it's a comfort to go hand in hand.

Emily Kimbrough

Whom it first crept into our lives, it was like a shadow that followed Mom around. Yet when the sun was shining, when *she* was shining, we were content to ignore it. But as Alzheimer's broke into my mother's brain and began to rewrite her life story, we had to confront the stranger. She has almost disappeared behind the veil of this thief now, but I remember those first few months. Mom's courage was unbelievable. She had seen her own mom, my sweet Granny, die from Alzheimer's disease, and when she put her head on the pillow at night, she used to ponder her fate. It must have scared the heck out of her to know that she was headed down that same dark hallway.

We used to sit down with a cup of coffee and talk about all the places we'd been, the people we loved and the moments we cherished. I call it our "soul-print." Mom's was vivid and clear. That's what makes us who we are, isn't it? That collection of life events like births and deaths, promises broken, dreams delivered, hearts crushed and hopes fulfilled. As Mom's memory became impaired, she lost the ability to recall the times that nourished and comforted her. She was frightened, agitated and inconsolable. It is like death in slow motion. My mother became vacant and hunched into herself.

I knew there was no way that I wanted that image to be what my kids remembered of my mom. I pored through old photos and tried to find the sepia-colored clues that could connect me to the seventeen-year-old girl who married my dad and had dreams much bigger than her small town. Those images led me to the ones that were "live and in living color"—the family years with a tri-level house and three kids. I devoured them all, and as my mother's memory faded, I became consumed with preserving her legacy in the pages of a scrapbook. I wanted to capture her essence and tell her story. In fact, it was my mother who helped me identify myself as a storyteller.

I was in the sixth grade, and there was a talent show at school. Uh-oh . . . I didn't have a talent! Girls were singing, playing piano and dancing. I had nothing. I came home from school crying, and my mother said to me, "Honey, you do have a talent. You're a storyteller. You're gonna stand up there in front of the class and tell your best story ever!"

Now I am telling the most important story of my life. It's about my family's battle with Alzheimer's disease. I use the pages of my scrapbooks to celebrate the moments that Mom has forgotten and to share with my family both the grand and humble events that make us who we are.

When my mother and father had their fiftieth wedding anniversary, my brother, sister and I didn't know what to do. We had always planned on a big event to memorialize the day, but now with Mom being so frail and Dad so depressed, it seemed like the wrong thing to do. *No, we thought, they are still married, and it is still an accomplishment—now more than ever.* So we planned a party and invited all the people who had loved them over the years.

Before the festivities, our family went by the skilled nursing facility to see Mom. We didn't know what to expect since sometimes having more than one person in the room was overwhelming to her. Daddy was dressed up in his best suit, and he arrived with a pink corsage for Mom. We kids had brought a cake and some music. It was "The Tennessee Waltz"—"their song." Mom looked particularly pathetic that day, hunched over and pulling at her shirt as she sat in a chair with not an ounce of recognition of the three children to whom she had given birth. Dad carefully pinned the corsage to her shirt, and we put on the music. The moment she heard it, Mom instantly reached up with her arms, got out of her chair and embraced my father. They were dancing as they had so many times over a half century. The song was so deeply embedded in the memory of her cells that Mom just went into that comforting place. Or maybe, just maybe, for that moment she got a kiss from the angels and was able to be present to experience a few seconds of a waltz.

As a gift for their wedding anniversary, my sister, Cammy, made them a scrapbook. All the guests who later offered congratulations to us had written letters and shared memories that Cam placed in the beautiful suede album. I think Daddy cried for days after he got it. I'm so happy that he has the pages to touch and share whenever he wants to.

Rewind a quarter of a century earlier at their twenty-fifth anniversary. Mom and Dad sat in front of a fire with champagne and the love letters they had written each other. They read the words aloud to each other, and after they had shared the letters, they threw each of them into the fire. Dad said at the time, "Those words are written in our hearts, and we will never forget them." How ironic that Mom can no longer remember her own love story. But still, a heart never forgets, and often when I see my mom, I know that love transcends experience.

"Honey, take my story. Tell it and make it count," my mother told me. I do that every day through my work with the Leeza Gibbons Memory Foundation. At our support centers, called Leeza's Place, one of our most popular activities is scrapbooking, where legacies, traditions and love are celebrated through pages. The experience has taught me to value every opportunity to tell others about this soul-satisfying hobby. A life well lived and people well loved deserve to live on. My mother was right; I am a storyteller, and my scrapbooks help me tell the tale of that sweet, strong, Southern woman whose rich life was stolen from her but still stands strong in my own memories.

Leeza Gibbons

With Sunlight Streaming In

Our brothers and sisters are there with us from the dawn of our personal stories to the inevitable dusk.

Susan Scarf Merrell

I was thirteen years old when my little brother arrived from Romania. I grew up as an only child, and then overnight I became a big sister to an adorable, ornery toddler. It seemed like JP had always been my little brother, even though I am older by twelve years. I was surviving middle school when he was learning to walk; I graduated from high school the year JP finished kinder-garten! Even with such a gap in our ages, there is one thing that we both enjoy—we love art! Creating art has become our special bond.

On weekends when I was still living at home, I would spread out all my scrapbook supplies on my pink-carpeted bedroom floor and scrap to my heart's content. At some point in the day, six-year-old JP would come wandering into my room, hands loaded with Lego creations. He would plop down on the floor in a big splash of sunshine and chatter away about all the things on his mind that day. Some days he didn't have much to say and would bring in his sheaf of typing paper and draw away. Other days he wanted to give me advice about what I should do with the scrapbook page I was working on. Every single time, though, he wanted to see the newest pages I had done, and he would "ooh" and "aah" over them, boosting my ego with his six-year-old praises.

Years passed and I went away to college, got married and moved into my own house. I wasn't around to have those long scrapbooking weekends with my little brother anymore. JP was visiting at my new house one day, and we had some time to spare, so we went up to my scrapbooking room. He asked to look through my most recent scrapbooks, so I pulled one out and we started looking through it. He had flipped through only a few pages when his eyes welled up with tears. He looked up at me and said in a small voice, "I miss you. I miss scrapbooking with you in your room, with the sunlight streaming in through the window . . ." and then his voice choked up.

I miss our precious weekend scrapbook days, too. We've managed to recreate them somewhat, with a few "scrapbook dates," but it's not quite the same as having unlimited, sunny afternoon hours together. But no matter how life changes for us, we will always have happy memories of pink carpet and sunshine, and we will always share that special love of creating and enjoying art with each other.

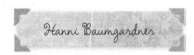

Hanni Baumgardner

A Wonderful Life

I love thee with the breath,
smiles, tears, of all my life!

Elizabeth Barrett Browning

As my parents' fiftieth anniversary approached, I took it upon myself as the oldest child to "take charge" of some of the plans. We wished to make our gift to them very special, and I came up with the idea of "50 Memories for 50 Years." I enlisted the help of my two brothers, my sister and our aunt to compile this list, knowing that between the five of us, it would be much easier. As the day approached, I gave some serious thought as to how we could present this. It was decided by my siblings that I should take the primary role and read the list at the party. But I was lucky enough to inherit the "crying" gene from my mother, and knowing that I tear up at the thought of anything sentimental, I recognized I would never get through the list in one piece. There had to be a way to convey our thoughts without me having to read them aloud in front of a crowd.

A friend of mine at work suggested a scrapbook. I had

been an amateur photographer since I was a child and always took pictures and saved them in scrapbooks. I would incorporate the souvenirs to tell the story. But I was not educated on the archival method of scrapbooking and had not yet been introduced to the "new trend" in scrapbooking. My friend helped me pick out the basics in albums and stickers and showed me some of her layouts as examples. I even found a magazine and a "how-to" book to get me started. Then I wandered into the local craft store and found aisles and aisles of supplies. I was suddenly a scrapbooker!

We all contributed photos from our own collections that spanned as far back as our parents' childhoods, dating years and high-school prom pictures. Wedding pictures were, of course, included, and photos of the early years of their marriage . . . through the early years of our family. We were so fortunate that our aunt had so many wonderful pictures from those early years, and I enlisted the help of my brother to surreptitiously go through all of my mother's scrapbooks from the last fifty years. I had requested each participant in our project to find ten pictures each in addition to the ten memories, and we finished with many more. As I put together this book over the next few weeks, it was as though I was reliving my own life.

Finally, it was done, just hours before we got on the plane to go "home" for the big party. This was a treasure to me, and I hand-carried it onto the plane, not trusting the airline with my hard work. I showed it to my brothers, sister and aunt before the party, and just before the guests arrived, I presented it to our parents. Tears came to my mother's eyes as she turned the pages, and I could see my father getting sentimental as well as he reminisced. I had prepared several pages for journaling of thoughts and memories from each guest, and the book was passed around the room during the party. I promised my mother that if she would send me the pictures taken at the party and return the book to me, I would finish it off, ending with the anniversary party.

My mother dutifully sent back the book and party pictures two months later, including a list of all the identities of the guests. And the book sat on my shelf . . . and sat for months and months, which turned into two years. Somehow my life got in the way of finding the time to finish it. That did not stop me from continuing to collect supplies, and more supplies. But amazingly I did not even start working on my own books. I just felt that I could never start my own work until I finished this book for my parents.

As summer was coming to a close that year, my father, who was suffering from cancer, was becoming weaker, and I worried that my planned visit that fall might be my last one. Somehow this gave me the impetus I needed, and I finished the scrapbook, page after page of the wonderful party that celebrated the fifty years of my parents' loving marriage. The final page was a family picture taken at the party. I was very proud of my work and of our family.

Once again, I hand-carried this treasure on the plane. By the time I arrived, my father had already been hospitalized and was clearly dying. But he was awake and alert and enjoying his family in what he knew would be his last days. The next afternoon, I carried the scrapbook to the hospital. You can imagine how heavy this scrapbook was by this time, and he could not hold it. But my husband and I stood next to his bed, holding the book so it would not weigh so heavily in his lap, and we turned each page. Once again, he relived his life from a young

child, to meeting and marrying his
high-school sweetheart, to raising four children,
watching us grow, graduate, marry and eventually
bear him grandchildren. The end of the book was, of
course, the fiftieth anniversary party, now two and a half
years past, but seeing the photos brought it back as fresh
in his mind as if it were yesterday. He lovingly looked at
every page, touching the pictures, lingering at many of
them, smiling and remembering, sometimes sharing,
sometimes in his own mind. I hated that we finally came
to the end, but as we turned the last page, my father looked
at me and said so softly, "I have had a wonderful life."

The next day my daddy went into a coma that finally
ended when he died two days later. I will always carry
with me that amazing memory of sharing with my daddy
at his end just a little of his wonderful life.

Merilyn J. Crittenden

I Never Thought

I believe it is the nature of people to be heroes, given the chance.

James A. Autry

Steve served twenty-two years in the Air Force and Air National Guard, so chances of his serving our country in Iraq were huge. We had been told there was a possibility of Steve's deployment earlier in the year. We knew it could happen, as it had happened for many already. Selfishly, I just wanted to keep Steve home safe with me and the kids. With the changes we were possibly facing, we were nervous to say the least. *How could I raise the boys by myself?* The fears and the unknowns were extremely overwhelming.

For fifteen years I had been a stay-at-home mom. Taking care of Steve and my sons was what I had lived for—as well as taking pride in making our house a home. Steve had a great job just a few minutes away in town. I will never forget the day he came home with all of his things in a little box. There had been cutbacks, downsizing. Steve no longer had a job or a place to care about his coworkers or a place to do more than collect a paycheck—it was a place that helped define him as Steve. It was more than a livelihood; it was his home away from home.

I went back into the workforce so we would at least have health insurance, and Steve hit the pavement looking for work. He worked for a temp agency hoping to get hired into a company, but the jobs in this area were slim to say the least. I couldn't help but feel that it was because he had National Guard on his résumé. We had even talked about getting out of the service so he could get a civilian job. Of course, not one potential employer would ever say that, but it was a reason why this caring and devoted man couldn't get a full-time job. His work ethics have always been strong, never missing work and putting the company's best interest first while he was working. In November 2004, the company Steve had been working for told him that they were going to offer him the job that he had been working as a temp. It looked like our life was going to be back to normal. Knowing that Christmas was just around the corner, we started to breathe a sigh of relief.

One month later, my fears were brought to reality. Steve came home from his weekend at the base with a letter for his new employer. He was going to be activated. His orders would be for at least a year. The rumor at the unit was Kuwait or Germany for six months, and maybe the other six months at a base here in the States. While most families, including ours, realize that this is part of being a military family, it never sinks in until it is real.

For the most part, we have a very traditional marriage, so how in the world do you prepare for the things you must take on? Steve has taken care of the finances, cars and lawn, and has always helped with whatever needed to be done. Now he was putting together a calendar of the following year for me so I would know when to change the furnace filter, add salt to the water softener and check the oil in the cars. Then he told me I would need to learn how to do the bills! Well, I cannot tell you how frightened I was of all of those things, but the one thing that had rattled me more than anything else was the fact that he would not be here. I have always said, "I cannot imagine a day that I couldn't breathe the same air that Steve does; he is the reason I am alive; he makes me a better me." His smile lights me up, inside and out. He is the wind beneath my wings. With his proven love, dedication and devotion, I know that I can do all things. He has always told me so!

I have always been proud of Steve, but now in this time that we are facing, I am even more so. To see half of your heart pack up everything he could take with him to serve our great nation for the freedom of others is a selfless act. To put your life on hold in order for others to have some of the same freedoms that we take for granted is so very humbling.

While I have learned how to take care of the everyday family activities, bills, household chores, and balancing career and kids . . . well, it has been a learning experience to say the least, and not one I wanted to embrace. But I have.

For a man to miss a year of his children's lives has been hard on all four of us. To help our children deal with the fact that Steve has been gone, we have been collecting all kinds of parts, pictures and memorabilia—as much as we can in order to put our lives all together for him for when he returns. We have chosen the scrapbooking album; the layouts are a work in progress every week. The boys feel good about being able to share their moments with Steve when he returns.

The healing aspects of this book of love and labor will go on for many generations to come. We have one life we lead; when we look back on our life, there should be things that stick out as monumental. We put this scrapbook together for Steve, hoping he'll always know what a hero he is to his children and adoring wife. It is dedicated to a hero, my hero, with love. It is the chapter in his life that he gave up in order to help others. It is from the heart and soul of the ones who love him the most—his family.

Debbie Haas

5

Overcoming Obstacles

One who gains strength by
overcoming obstacles possesses
the only strength which can
overcome adversity.

Albert Schweitzer

Reconciliation

How often could things be remedied by a word? How often is it left unspoken?

Norman Douglas

I was twenty-three and my two younger sisters, Charlotte and Carmen, were seventeen and sixteen, respectively, when our mother passed away. She was a single mom and our "rock" when she passed away from complications of leukemia. Almost immediately afterward, all of our lives spiraled out of control. Being the oldest, I tried to take over the role of "Mom," but failed miserably, and after some time we found ourselves spread out across the country living separate lives and barely communicating.

Through the years, including marriages and divorces, children being born and all the years in-between, I found myself longing for a relationship with my sisters, but I did not know how to go about any kind of reconciliation until I walked into a local scrapbook store. As I looked around at all of the wonderful layouts on display, I had an over-whelming desire to make memory books of Momma for my sisters. It was my way of reaching out to them and hopefully reconnecting. I knew we couldn't get back what we had lost, but we could start over with God's help.

As the weeks went by and I painstakingly worked on these memory books, praying over each page, God was healing my heart in a way that I had not experienced before. I don't think I had ever really grieved for my mother completely, and this was a way that allowed it to happen so that I could totally give my hurt to God and let it go.

Mother's Day was approaching, so I finished both albums and mailed them to my sisters. I was a bit on edge wondering how they would be received—neither Charlotte nor Carmen have ever been good at showing emotion or excitement about much of anything. I think I got all those genes, so I wasn't really expecting much of a response, to be honest.

A few days after I mailed the albums, Charlotte called. She actually scared me because she was crying so hard that I couldn't understand her, and then she calmed down and told me how much the memory book meant to her. God began restoring our relationship that very moment. We have been sharing our lives for five years now—the good, the bad and the ugly—but we are sisters once again, and I can only give the glory to God for this.

Carmen called a day later, and she was bawling and saying much the same as Charlotte. We have now formed a wonderful relationship, and I've also made two scrapbooks of her boys for her.

I thank God for the way he has worked in all of our lives, and now I'm being blessed with teaching my sister Charlotte the basics of scrapbooking. I look forward to forming an even deeper bond with her through this great hobby.

Cindy Lee Sparks

A Tribute

Let the healing grace of your love,
O Lord, so transform me that I may
play my part in the transfiguration
of the world from a place of suffering,
death and corruption to a realm of
infinite light, joy and love.

Martin Israel

I can still remember that day as if it were yesterday. Life was returning to normal after a long Labor Day holiday weekend. The air was warm, the sky was a brilliant shade of blue with white puffy clouds—all was normal and happy. After dropping the kids off at school, I was finally indulging myself with a Christmas gift my husband gave to me nine months earlier—a day of beauty with the works. I spent three long, luxurious hours loving every second of my pampering. I left the salon after noon and drove away in sheer bliss. Stopping by a friend's store to say hello became a rude awakening to the reality of life, for on the television were the pictures of the World Trade

Center crumbling to the ground. The once blue sky was filled with darkness. In shock and fear I rushed home, not fully comprehending what had happened and what events would take place in my life. Thinking we were at war in my own backyard and perhaps the world was ending, I tried to call everyone I knew to tell them that I loved them.

Over the days following 9/11, I clung to the TV, waiting for news. I read everything the newspapers printed. I waited in long lines to give blood, only to be turned away because the centers were so overwhelmed. I collected food and clothing with my family to send to the rescue workers at ground zero. I clung to my husband and my children . . . and I prayed. Letting my husband go into Manhattan to help with the rescue and recovery efforts proved to be a difficult struggle with my inner strength. Every time the phone rang, I would hold my breath, waiting to hear the tearful voice on the other end saying who we knew that was missing and who we knew that was found—either deceased or living. Daily functioning proved to be a very difficult task.

Wakes and funerals started. Seeing two fire trucks draped in American flags became a common sight, as well as the droning sound of the bagpipes. In the twenty-two years my husband had served on the NYPD, I had never seen him in his police uniform so much. The sadness on his face every time he dressed for a funeral, and the tears in his eyes every time he returned, broke my heart over and over. The pain was real and strong. I experienced it firsthand when I learned that my cousin FF Eric T. Olsen and my childhood friend FF Richard Muldowney were missing—later to be declared deceased.

I remember asking my mother what she remembered from the attacks on Pearl Harbor; her response was, "Not much, I was a small child." At that moment I made a silent vow that neither I nor my children would ever forget the events of September 11, 2001. Unfortunately, this was now a part of history. I decided that someday I would create a scrapbook to reflect the good and the bad that came from this terrible event. Here and there over time, I would collect bits of memorabilia, poems, newspaper clippings and even photos. Each day I would think about starting this album, but my grief was too large to sit down and actually do it.

On the first anniversary of 9/11, as my husband went into the city for the services, I settled down to watch it on television. As my heart filled with sorrow once again, I thought I would never heal. It was then that I set my table up in front of the TV with all of my 9/11 paraphernalia and started my tribute album. Through tears I created tasteful pages that recollected the actual events of the day, depicting my pages in red, white, blue and black. I documented everything. Once I got past the actual moments of the day, I moved on to creating memorial pages of family and friends we had lost. I recorded my feelings, my children's feelings and my husband's, too. In most of the book, however, I wanted to capture the good that came out of human nature. I included things like patriotism, strangers helping strangers, volunteers collecting blood, food, clothing and money, mostly people coming together for the good of man.

I remember lighting candles and setting them on my front porch the Friday after 9/11 happened. The skies had just cleared after a short rainstorm. As we lit the candles and set them out, a rainbow appeared. It reminded me of God's promise after the flood in the book of Genesis. I thought to myself that maybe this was God's way to remind us of his promise, and he would not let something like this happen again. It was in a sense a step toward the healing process, just as I found creating this scrapbook had helped me to heal as well. After three and a half years, I have, in a large sense, accepted what happened on that fateful day, but I will never forget. As each anniversary passes, we will light a candle on our doorstep and solemnly look through the scrapbook, remembering those who have gone on. And one day when my grandchildren ask me what I remember about the historical day of 9/11, I will be able to show them what we all experienced—the good, the bad and the power of healing.

Allison Connors

The Healing Journey

Death leaves a heartache no one can heal;
love leaves a memory no one can steal.

Author Unknown

My husband and I had just started trying to have a baby, and the desire was so strong. When I had seen the doctor for my yearly checkup, she seemed convinced that we would probably experience difficulty in conceiving a child. We were amazed when I got pregnant so quickly and thrilled to the depths of our souls. We told all of our family and friends, and we even began purchasing items for that new little someone. To our dismay, the pregnancy terminated itself right at the end of our first trimester. We were devastated. The baby that we were looking so forward to meeting one day was cruelly snatched from our grasp. I did not know how to express my grief for this child whom we never got to meet, and I could feel the despair taking over my heart.

To make matters worse, I worked in a day-care setting at that time, and I was surrounded by teen moms who did not even want their children. Day in and day out, I went through the motions of daily life, feeling empty and broken inside. My husband and I never discussed the baby or the pregnancy. Then one day I ran across an article in one of my scrapbooking magazines that talked about scrapbooking the bad things of life as well as the good things. In that article was a layout about a woman who had fertility problems and suffered multiple miscarriages. She had endured those heartaches and found comfort in scrapbooking about her heart-wrenching disappointments. I dog-eared that page. It had never occurred to me to use something so heartbreaking in an album before. But there before my eyes, I saw my pain mirrored in someone else's layout. As I thought of doing just as this woman had done, the pain eased a bit. By making a layout about my miscarriage, I would then make my child a memory.

So many people did not understand why I grieved over a child I had never met. This would make that child human, in a sense. While I planned for my layout, we found out that I was pregnant again. We were happy, but so very scared. My husband and I decided to tell only our parents and a few close friends this time, and that proved to be the smart thing to do. Once again, at that same stage of pregnancy, I miscarried. I put all thoughts of a layout about my baby aside, for the pain was too fresh. I had never healed from the first loss, so I felt I could not face the second. My babies were gone, and I never had the chance to hold them. One day, months later, I found myself searching for that article again. I read through the woman's journaling, and I felt a resolve come over me. I would make my layout in honor of my lost lambs. As I planned the pages, I felt excitement mix with the pain in my heart. My children would be honored. They would not just disappear into nothingness.

The hard part was yet to come—the journaling. I avoided writing about the experience at all costs, but to no avail. One night I found myself unable to sleep, with thoughts of my little ones filling my mind. I climbed out of bed and went to my chair, notebook and pen in hand. There I wrote a beautiful song in honor of my first baby, Micah Christian. As exhausted as I was, sleep would not come. All I could think about was how to make sure that my babies were not forgotten. I had my song for Micah, but what about my little Charity Noel? I drifted in and out of consciousness until the idea hit me.

In my mind, I had been constructing a letter to my little girl. Why not put it on paper? Hours later, I crawled into my bed exhausted emotionally as well as physically. I found that as I wrote my song and letter and expressed my feelings for my lost children, the darkness began to subside from my heart. I could feel the sadness as the tears coursed down my cheeks; I could still sense the utter loss. But my children would be remembered even after I was gone. They would be part of a legacy. People would know that they existed. If it had not been for scrapbooking, that healing journey would have never begun. I was not instantly better, but I was able to move forward from that moment and see all that life had to offer me. I learned that scrapbooking is not just for pleasure, but it is also for pain. Scrapbooking is a type of therapy. Now my little hobby means so much more to me than before. It is not just about reminiscing on paper, but making memories for those who otherwise would have never been known.

Melissa Tharp

Keepsake of My Heart

Inner peace is beyond victory or defeat.

Bhagavad Gita

My husband didn't understand.

"Why now?" he asked, confused. The scrapbook page I was working on wasn't of our infant daughter, precocious toddler or teenage son. It was a page in honor of the baby I'd lost two years earlier to miscarriage.

"I need something tangible to honor my memories," I offered as an explanation. The subject made him uncomfortable—rightfully so. The days following our loss were some of the darkest in my life. My grief was torrential and very private. Sympathy only deepened my wound. I was unable to accept it, especially since I already had two healthy children. Who was I to grieve this way when there are women who will never have a child? I felt ashamed of my grief—afraid that I was ungrateful for the many blessings in my life. The few reminders, like the skirt I'd worn to the fateful ultrasound appointment, had been discarded as I'd tried to gain some control during an uncontrollable event. We were blessed with a healthy pregnancy immediately following the miscarriage, and my tears were replaced with unfounded fears for the new baby's safety. I felt guilty mourning my loss and accepting my new blessing at the same time. The miscarriage was swept under the rug.

One day as I was journaling about my darling baby, Olivia, my thoughts turned to my lost baby instead. I started to write—not the pages I'd wrung out from the bottom of my soul before—but words of tribute. I decided to do a full-fledged layout. Simple papers, pens, ink, words and trinkets became magical devices. Subconsciously, I created a very symbolic layout. I was finally able to use my sister's dramatic photo of the sky—storm clouds and a ray of sunshine—to symbolize hope. The snow-white silk shantung was innocence and purity. The clear beads were my tears. The torn, textured papers were my pain. A shadowy, translucent image of a woman stamped on mica, her arms empty, her gaze forlorn, was a self portrait, I suppose.

On occasion, someone opens this page of my scrapbook, and there is a silent understanding and sometimes tears. My hobby gave an outlet for my lingering grief to escape. I was able to revisit the devastation and explore it from a new perspective. I allowed myself to mourn without guilt. There were fresh tears . . . new sorrow . . . and, finally, peace.

Kelley Crisanti

A Random Act of Kindness

Miss no single opportunity of making some small sacrifice, here by a smiling look, there by a kindly word; always doing the smallest right and doing it all for love.

St. Thérèse of Lisieux

In 2004, my sister and our parents moved from their hometown of Atlanta to the medical "mecca" of Pittsburgh so that my sister could undergo a small intestinal transplant for a life-threatening disease she had been battling since birth. The three of them lived at Family House, a "home away from home" for patients and their families who travel to Pittsburgh to receive medical treatment.

While my family quickly made some amazing friends at the house, their stay in Pittsburgh became much longer than originally expected due to complications in my sister's recovery. People were incredibly supportive of my sister—she received cards and trinkets of encouragement daily. But I began to worry about my mom. She became withdrawn and really worn down by the slow progress my sister made. Wanting to cheer her up, my husband and I drove from our home outside of Philadelphia for a weekend visit.

Knowing how much I enjoy my scrapbooking and card-making hobbies, I took along all the supplies I could fit into the car. I was on a mission to cheer up my mom through the therapeutic use of crafts. I didn't know if she would show any interest in it, but to my surprise we stayed up until we made cards of every size and color! I hadn't seen my mom so vibrant in quite a while. I took her to the craft store the next day to pick up a few things to help get her started on her newfound hobby. Her first goal was to make all of her Christmas cards that year. When I left that weekend, I was encouraged because I knew I was leaving behind a creative way for my mom to spend her time while helping my sister recover.

My mom and I began having long conversations over the phone to discuss techniques related to card making, and we exchanged e-mails notifying each other of upcoming sales at the local craft stores. It had been quite some time since I had felt so connected to my mom, and it was a great feeling.

Unfortunately, my mom really had to budget herself in buying supplies since my sister's medical bills had to come first. And as any craft fiend knows, taking up any hobby related to paper crafting can become an expensive habit. So I turned to a group of women who understand the love of this art more than anyone—the ladies at *www.twopeasinabucket.com* message board.

I had received and sent out a few Random Acts of Kindness through this message board, and knew I could count on them to help my mom. I posted a message explaining the situation and asked anyone who had spare supplies, such as extra sheets of stickers, to send them to my mom in Pittsburgh. I knew that not only could my mom use the supplies, but she could really use the encouragement of letters and good wishes.

Within a matter of days, I got a call from my mom telling me that she had received a really nice package of craft supplies from a stranger, and she asked if I knew who it was from. I let her in on the post I had made on the message board, and she was so surprised. She was incredibly happy to get that first package; she had been making cards every night since I left and had just about run out of supplies!

From that point on, the response was overwhelming. My mom began receiving cards, letters and packages full of supplies and, most importantly, inspiration. The next visit I made to Pittsburgh was even more uplifting. My mom and I hosted a very successful craft night with a few of the other Family House guests. I took my supplies, and mom hauled out all the goodies she had received from the ladies at Two Peas to share with our new friends. It felt so good to bond with my mom and the other women and to hear the halls of that house echo with laughter. That night my mom discovered a love for scrapbooking and began to document the transplant experience that my sister and our family were sharing.

We have all seen a change in my mom since the first night I sat down and introduced this incredible hobby to her. Hearing her appreciation each day that she received a package full of new goodies brought tears to my eyes. The women at Two Peas had brightened a dark time in my mom's life, had reaffirmed my faith in the kindness of strangers and had planted the seeds for a new beginning for my relationship with my mom. I can never say thank you enough to those incredible women for helping nurture a new spirit within my mom and for bringing me even closer to her.

After nearly ten months in Pittsburgh, my sister and parents are now back home in Atlanta. My sister has a new chance at life thanks to her transplant, and my mom has a new passion for life other than my sister's illness. We spoke just yesterday, and I listened with a huge, grateful smile as my mom described her plans to convert the guest room in the house I grew up in into her very own craft room. We have a lot to be thankful for these days and many more memories to scrapbook in the future!

Jessica LaGrossa

Christmas in March

And as to me, I know of nothing else but miracles.

Walt Whitman

C hristmas 2003 began like all others. On December 15, my tree was up, most of the presents were bought and wrapped, and our outside light display was only a few bulbs shy of Clark Griswold's in the movie *Christmas Vacation*. But on December 16 my world turned upside down when my healthy daughter, Jennifer, suddenly found herself paralyzed and unable to walk. With no warning or reason, her body was rapidly turning into stone.

After extensive testing dismissed all of the common causes for this sudden paralysis, Jennifer was diagnosed with Guillain-Barré Syndrome (GBS). This autoimmune illness is characterized by the rapid onset of paralysis of the legs, arms, breathing muscles and face. We learned that GBS was very rare, only one case per one hundred thousand. What made our situation even more dramatic was the fact that Jennifer was six months pregnant. The specialists in Dallas had never encountered this combination.

After reviewing the medical journals, they discovered only a handful of such cases had ever been documented.

Jennifer immediately underwent treatment, but her condition worsened. The paralysis that had begun in her legs moved up her body until she was totally paralyzed head to toe. By Christmas evening, we were terrified the medicine was not working and that she would lose her ability to breathe on her own. My strong faith had held me to this point, but that Christmas night was the worst moment in my life—I realized that my daughter could die.

The treatment finally stopped the progression of the paralysis, and on January 8 Jennifer was moved to rehabilitation. Unfortunately, this move resulted in the onset of premature labor. So, on January 11 my daughter became the first recorded case of a totally paralyzed GBS patient to give birth naturally, assisted only by forceps. Because Jennifer had GBS, she could not receive an epidural, and even though she was paralyzed, she could still feel pain. The human body is a marvelous creation. My daughter could barely breathe, couldn't talk, couldn't move anything from head to toe, had just regained her ability to close her eyelids, and somehow her body managed to deliver a baby!

So, on this Sunday afternoon, four-pound Presley Brooke Galitz entered our lives two months ahead of schedule. As an avid photographer and scrapbooker, I had long dreamed of the day when I would become a grandmother. In anticipation, I started a journal the day we discovered Jennifer was pregnant. Every trip to the craft store resulted in new pink baby papers and sweet embellishments for my special scrapbook devoted to all of the happy days I planned to spend in my new role as "Nana." I just never imagined those days would begin in a neonatal intensive care unit. I was elated that my granddaughter had arrived safely, but saddened that my daughter could not see her due to her blurred vision, could not kiss her because her face was paralyzed, and could not hold her until she was almost a month old.

Presley's birth wreaked havoc on Jennifer's body, and instead of going back to rehab, she was sent to ICU. Jennifer lost her ability to swallow and was put on a feeding tube. Each day we feared that she would succumb to the final blow and lose her ability to breathe unassisted. Faith prevailed, and after three weeks in intensive care, Jennifer was deemed strong enough to reenter rehab.

Many scrapbookers edit their memories. For whatever reason, they determine which stories will go down in their albums and which ones will be forgotten. As family historians, we know the value of these books; we understand how fragile our memories are and how easily time erases them. Sometimes it hurts to remember; sometimes we want to forget.

When my daughter got sick, my family entered a new world. Every day, I felt like I was trapped in a bad made-for-TV movie. Most of my family and friends were horrified when they saw my camera. How could I even consider photographing any part of this living nightmare? To me, these moments, no matter how painful, were very important. Each night before I fell asleep in the awful green chair next to Jennifer's hospital bed, I forced myself to chronicle the day's events. These pictures and words recorded our tragedy, but they also lit the way to Jennifer's recovery.

On days when Jennifer lost hope, when she could see no progress, my notes revealed every small success. "On Tuesday you couldn't hold a straw between your lips, but today you can!" "Last week it took us ten minutes to transfer you to your wheelchair, but now we manage in five."

What might appear as morbid notations can also be interpreted as miracles in progress.

Jennifer made amazing progress. At first we prayed that she would progress to a wheelchair by the time Presley was due to leave the neonatal ICU. But on March 11, when Jennifer and Presley left the hospital together, Jennifer could walk with crutches! My daughter had entered the hospital in the dead of winter, but was finally leaving at the dawn of spring.

Two days later, our family gathered around a Christmas tree with dusty packages beneath. Outside the wooden reindeers were still standing next to Santa's sleigh. Undaunted by the sounds of distant lawn mowers and Weed Eaters, we sang carols, opened presents, shot five rolls of film, overate all of our favorite holiday treats and had our traditional family Christmas—in March.

When you assume the role of family historian, you initially focus on the happy, triumphant moments. It is easy to chronicle most of the important events in your life, to collect certificates of honor and love letters, to photograph your family gathered around a lush Thanksgiving Day feast. What is not so easy is to photograph your once happy and healthy family gathered around a hospital bed.

Today, when I see my daughter laughing and running after her toddler, it seems like this never happened. Thankfully, both of them are healthy and no telltale signs remain. But we do have our scrapbook. One day, when Presley is older, we will be able to sit down and tell her the amazing story of her mother's strength and courage that resulted in the miracle of her birth.

Cathy Arnold

Creating a Legacy of Love

Perhaps they are not stars in the sky, but rather openings where our loved ones shine down to let us know they are happy.

Eskimo Legend

In the summer of 1996, my family and I moved into a new neighborhood. One of the first people I met was Brenda. She had just had her third child and so had I, both girls. We spent a lot of time together. Our children were growing up alongside each other and becoming the best of friends. We had Bible studies together, family Easter egg hunts, picnics in the backyard and days at the park. I came to think of Brenda as one of my best friends.

In 2000, Brenda was diagnosed with ovarian cancer. It was a devastating blow to all of us who knew and loved her. Over the next three and a half years, she fought through chemo to remission, back to chemo and then radiation.

Finally, she was told there was nothing more that could be done.

For the last months of her life, Brenda began to set the things of this life in order. Knowing that she wouldn't be there for the important days of her children's lives, she wanted to do some special things for them that would help them remember her love when those days came. High on her list was to make sure that her children's memory books were up-to-date. It was a way of leaving a legacy for her children that would outlive her and give them a tangible expression of her love. It was a way of saying good-bye. Unfortunately, as her condition worsened, she was no longer able to sit long enough to work on them.

As a way to minister to this dear sister I loved, I took on the job of finishing her scrapbooks. It was a blessing I could not have foreseen. We would pore over her pictures, many of which included my family as well, and the memories would flood back. We would talk about where this took place and where that happened. It was a journey of healing and hope for two friends on a road that we both knew would lead us to an all-too-soon good-bye. It was a journey I would not have traded for the world.

I managed to get the majority of the pictures in the

books, which became very special to all of her children. Brenda's hope was that her labor of love would inspire her children to continue what she had begun—capturing memories in a way that carries them to the future.

Brenda has been gone for a year now. I miss her still. I find myself reaching for the phone to share a bit of news or a silly story from one of my children. Instead, I say a prayer for her family, realizing my loss is only a small seed compared to their loss. Now our photos are a place to stop and visit . . . a place to go over those memories that we laughed and cried about while we sorted through pictures.

We created a legacy in those few short months, a reminder of hope and love shared with those who are left when we have to go on ahead. I'm thankful for the opportunity I was given to take part in its creation. Through those scrapbooks, her legacy of love lives on.

Brenda Falk

Winter Crows

Our problem is not to be rid of fear,
but rather to harness and master it.

Martin Luther King, Jr.

O n the morning of March 20, the vernal equinox, our family life was about to be changed forever. It was a brisk and eerie morning when my mother found a lump in her left breast. She immediately headed to the doctor's office alone. Deep down she knew it was bad and didn't want her children and granddaughter to learn of it just yet. At home, while praying and hoping for the best, the three of us girls huddled together waiting for some news. Then, suddenly, the crows arrived. With deafening, earsplitting screeching, they made their presence known to us. Hundreds of them landed in our large maple trees simultaneously. The excruciating sound was almost unbearable. My daughter covered her ears with both hands as I tried to comfort her. What are they? Why were they here? What do they want from us? We were frightened by these birds that we hadn't encountered before. If the fear of Mom's news wasn't enough, we were now being terrorized by an unfamiliar group of strangers in our own backyard.

Being the scrapbooker that I am, without hesitation, I quickly grabbed my camera. I snapped a few photos of the scary black birds, all the while trying not to drop the camera from my trembling hands. The fright that ran through me was overcome by the desire to record this incident. My own fear of birds since childhood departed from me for a brief moment of courage. Then they left as suddenly as they had arrived. It was almost as if they had magically disappeared in the snap of a camera lens. They left with such force, you could hear the "swoosh" of their wings. It sounded similar to a jet taking off. They were gone.

The silence was stifling—until the phone rang—and in an instant I knew our world was crashing down. It was confirmed. Mom had cancer. At that precise moment in the doctor's office, as scared as she was, Mom needed to make a brave decision. She did, and within days she had a complete mastectomy.

Over the next few months, we watched and worried as Mom went through daily chemotherapy and radiation. As difficult as it was for me, I realized just how important it was to document her illness with both photos and journaling. I needed to console myself within my scrapbooks and my own accounts of her illness and this journey where life was taking all of us. Mom never showed any signs of a side effect, fear or weakness. She drove herself daily to the oncologist's office for treatment. She refused to give in to the illness and let it take over her body. She bought herself a wig and went out during this ordeal, living her life as usual. I asked if I could photograph her without her hair for the scrapbook, and she agreed without hesitation.

Just a week before she found the lump, she gathered us all together for a family portrait. Funny, it was as if she knew something was about to happen and wanted to have a formal picture for the family. These days, I look back upon that portrait quite often. I realize that no one had any idea of what was to come, or that Mom's thick and shiny silver hair, as recorded in that photograph, was about to be gone.

Soon after we were faced with the news of my mother's illness, I was watching a documentary on television about birds. I discovered that these horrific birds are called "winter crows." They travel in groups of two hundred, sometimes more. The flocks fly from town to town together; no one knows why. The documentary stated that people fear impending doom when they see these crows arrive—I can certainly attest to that firsthand. I now know why the winter crows stopped at our house on that March day.

Mom has since fully recovered by the grace of God and has remained in remission for five years now. She has been an incredible role model for us all. By letting me photograph her at her darkest moment, she ensured that her granddaughter will know what happened. And thanks to my scrapbooks she will know the feelings behind them. She will know the fear I felt as depicted in my least favorite page titled "Winter Crows." She will also know the pride I felt through my favorite page called "Thrive and Survive." This page reflects photos of Mom fully bald, as well as with her hair regrown, just as shiny and silver as ever before. She won over her fear. She made it. I realize now that both Mom and I faced a fear that day, and we made it through together.

Patricia Nelson

I Didn't Ask for Seconds

If you ever get a second chance at life, you've got to go all the way.

Lance Armstrong

Just when I thought my plate was overflowing with more than my share of problems, another heaping was ladled onto the dish. Wait a minute! I didn't ask for seconds! Really, I am on a trauma-free diet, so thank you, but I'm full. Unfortunately in life, our concerns aren't allocated fairly. Sometimes we experience so much grief that we actually can feel our hearts splinter under the crushing weight of sadness. Recently, my three-year-old son, Cole, was diagnosed with leukemia, and my family's world shattered into a million shards of unrecognizable pain.

Cole was our healthy child, our energetic and mischievous rascal who rallied around his older, special-needs sister, Sophie. It was Sophie who spent her first days in the ICU. It was Sophie who has so many doctors that I need a spreadsheet program to remember who is who. But not Cole! Not my baby boy. Please tell me my sweet, precious Coley does not have CANCER! I remember the pediatrician barely meeting my eyes as he, a friendly yet stoic man, choked on the word "leukemia." I sobbed and sobbed until I thought there was nothing left inside to feel. Boy, was I wrong.

We were told to pack our bags and go to the emergency room at Boston Children's Hospital where they were awaiting our arrival. During the hour-long drive to the city, my husband and I trembled and faltered, trying to find appropriate, comforting words. I know the only thought I could muster was *cancer equals death*. Desperately, I attempted to chase such an idea away with fervent prayers. We must trust God! He runs the show, and he is in control. Somehow, despite these truths I wholeheartedly believed, only rage surfaced. How dare he do this to Cole, to us? Where is his mercy? I ranted like a toddler having a tantrum. It wasn't pretty.

Inside the hospital I caught a glimpse of myself in a mirror and gasped at the woman staring back at me. Surely that wretched creature was not ME! My eyes were bloodshot and swollen, my cheeks blotchy and wet from tears. And why is it that one can never have a good hair day amid a crisis? Let's not even talk about the oh-so-attractive runny nose I wiped on my sleeve. I think Cole was more scared of my appearance than the needle-wielding nurse; nonetheless, it was strange how I found some semblance of peace at the most unlikely time in the most unlikely place (the hospital bathroom, for goodness sake!). As I studied my frightful face, I knew that although we were in for a long haul, we would eventually survive this ordeal. So like God to send me serenity via a glamour "don't!"

Three months have passed since Cole's diagnosis (five weeks of which were spent in inpatient care), and by God's mercy, Cole is in remission. I must declare that I have felt every emotion known to man as well as a few others I invented. During the impossibly lengthy stay in the luxurious oncology ward at Children's, I began an online journal that friends and family could access for updates. These entries, however, became so much more than briefings on Cole's condition. They embodied my despair and hope, my longings and fears. In essence, they were my means for coping, my thrifty therapy! But I want to remember this roller-coaster ride, and more importantly, I want Cole to know just how courageous he was during his radiation treatments and spinal taps and bone marrow tests. I have the makings of a truly inspiring celebration of life, which will be immortalized in a very special scrapbook my entire family can cherish. And I know that this book will have a very happy ending.

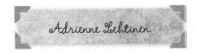

Adrienne Lehtinen

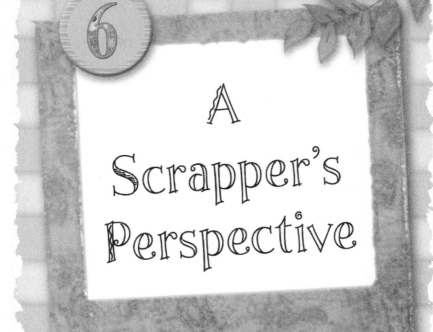

A Scrapper's Perspective

Scrapbooking isn't
about scraps of paper and photos.
Scrapbooking is about scraps of life—
yours and those special to you.

Rebecca Sower

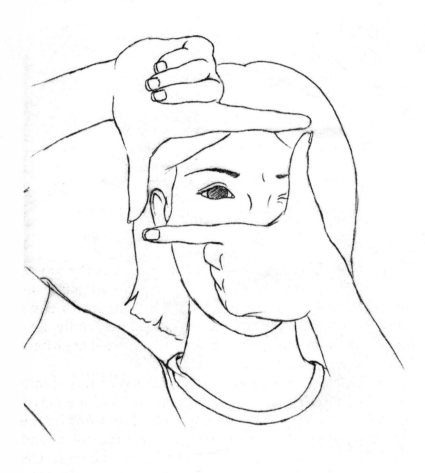

Reprinted by permission of Mack Dobbie ©2005.

Please Promise Me

I believe the true function of age is memory. I am recording as fast as I can.

Rita Mae Brown

Please promise me that if I ever forget, really forget, you'll remind me—often—of my life, of our lives together. Please promise to tell me who you are if I don't seem to know. Please be patient and tell me kindly, lovingly and as often as I ask. Please promise to tell me where I have been, where we have been together.

Show me my scrapbooks. I put so much of myself into them—surely they will spark recognition and memories in my heart of hearts. Tell me the stories I recorded on the pages I crafted. My handwriting, my favorite colors and yours. Tell me who the people are in the pictures. The stories and the photographs are more important than the art, although I enjoyed the creating part so, so much. Laugh with me as you show me. Let me touch them.

I have a fear. I fear forgetting, not having my memory someday. I cry as I write this—and I don't cry easily—

because the thought of being abandoned by my memories is terrifying. I can't imagine a lonelier existence than living without memories. So many of my scrapbooking friends say they are scrapping for their children and grandchildren. I do, too, but honestly, I am also scrapping for myself—because I am afraid of forgetting.

I know you will have your own full lives—husbands, wives, children, ministries, jobs, education—all of those things that I spent so many years preparing you for. I don't want to be a burden, ever—really I don't. I can't imagine that anyone would want that for herself. But please promise me that if I should ever need it, you will help me to remember. If I seem like I have forgotten, just please promise you'll try.

I forget so much these days. I am only thirty-seven. Is it just because I have a new baby, a busy toddler and two homeschooled girls? Or is it because my mind can hold no more? Is it a symptom? Probably not. I am probably just overloaded with information, activity, interruptions and sweet life. But just in case, in case it's a symptom, an indicator of memory loss to come, I wanted to get this on paper. My plea—please promise me.

Stacey Kingman

Our Scrapbook Journey

Time is a companion that goes with us on a journey. It reminds us to cherish each moment because it will never come again. What we leave behind is not as important as how we have lived.

From the film Star Trek: Generations

L et's go!" I hollered to the kids for the third time in the last five minutes.

We were headed out to do the grocery shopping and several other errands on that warm, summer morning before it got too late and too hot. It was midmorning—half the day was already gone.

I sighed exasperatedly, slowly blowing the air from my puffed cheeks. Why do they have to mess around and go so slowly? Can't they just hurry up and help get the job done?

Giggling floated down the stairs from the older two kids. They were in the middle of a hilarious tale about their friends—part fiction and part truth. Meanwhile, the youngest was yelling "Aaahhh!" as he chased the cats around and around the loop that made up our first level.

"The sooner we go, the sooner we get back," I called for good measure. "Jennifer and Joshua, stop talking long enough to come down here so that we can go. Eric, leave those poor cats alone."

I sighed again. If they were just a little bit older, I could leave them at home. Just imagine, grocery shopping by myself. Imagine? I couldn't even remember the last time I had a moment alone to go to the bathroom. How could I fathom what it was like going somewhere solo?

On the way past my bed, I stopped long enough to turn off my laptop. After all, at this rate, it would take all day to get our work done. No sense leaving my computer on that long. I shook my head and rolled my eyes in frustration. But before I could move the cursor to begin the shutdown, something on the screen caught my eye.

Jennifer, in her teal and green flowing dance outfit, graced my screen. Her arms were poised perfectly in a ballerina stance as she performed her first solo. She looked so beautiful—her expression so reverent. I remembered the hard work and extra practices she put in to prepare the selection as a surprise for her daddy. The song she chose was one of his favorites.

As her picture faded, Joshua entered the screen in his pale blue jersey with his hands on his hips and his left foot atop the soccer ball. He wore his biggest, proudest grin. Oh, how he loves that sport and being with his friends!

Then a lion came creeping into view. It was Eric dressed for Halloween on our Disney cruise. The picture had captured him off guard, not in his usual posed position with a forced smile. His true personality shined, outlined and enhanced by a long-haired mane encircling his young face.

The slide show continued, picture after picture. Each one brought back a special memory. Some made me laugh. Others brought tears to my eyes.

Suddenly, I was pulled from my reverie. Each child in turn called, "Mommy!" Our three dark-haired, stair-stepped children appeared in the doorway. I turned to look at them from my perch on the bed, tears still glistening in my eyes. When had I sat down? I couldn't recall. How long had I been watching the faces pass?

"What are you doing? I thought we were leaving,"  Joshua stated matter-of-factly.

Concern crossed my oldest child's face. "What's wrong?" she asked, her head tilted as she does when worried.

Eric, with no words at all, merely crossed the room, climbed onto the bed, leaned against me and watched the screen. Soon the other two joined us. We arranged our-selves comfortably for the duration: cross-legged, two on their knees, and the third resting against me with his legs dangling over the edge of the bed.

"Aw!" they said as each picture appeared. "I remember that. . . ."

The time passed along with the pictures. Memories cruised before us, one-by-one. Those errands didn't seem nearly as important anymore. And the "hurry up and go" had long since gone. For that day, in those moments, the four of us were creating another page on our scrapbook journey.

Paula F. Blevins

Don't Sweat the Small Stuff—Scrap It!

I am beginning to learn that it is the sweet, simple things of life which are the real ones after all.

Laura Ingalls Wilder

I love holidays. I look forward to them differently than just any old day. If you ask my husband, I go more than a little crazy at Christmas, and we always make a big deal out of birthdays in our family. Of course, being the shutterbug that I've become, there are always dozens of photos left to enjoy.

But my scrapbooks tell other stories of more ordinary moments. Stories of piles of laundry as high as the dryer; of peek-a-boo games with my six-month-old; of pancakes with maple syrup on lazy Sunday mornings; of dirty little boys and their Tonka trucks on a lethargic June afternoon; of dainty little girls and their pink toenails; of chubby babies, peacefully sleeping, swaddled in an heirloom quilt; of disappointments and frustration; of tears, both happy and sad; of us, exactly as we are, and stories we will remember and cherish, for they are a part of who we are. These are the stories that capture our life, our family, our world, our history.

Scrapbooking has brought so much texture to my life. I used to grumble as I swept up after the kids, gathering crumbs of Play-Doh and used stickers up off the floor; now I photograph it and archive these "crumbs of childhood." I used to dread the coming of frosty winter days with the days ending so early; now I journal on my winter pages, memorializing the richness of the cocoa, the coziness of the crackling fire. I used to tear out my hair as the laundry mounted, spilling over the tops of the baskets and out of the laundry room into the hall; now I create the perfect photo shoot with a two-year-old and let her roll around in it, snapping away as she feels the different textures, explores the vivid colors and enjoys the simple abandon.

When I quit sweating the details, the small stuff of life, and let my camera and my children guide me through my own world, I can enjoy the great abundance in my life— the abundance of laughter, color, blessings and joy. So when I find myself worrying, stressing and complaining, that's my signal: grab the kids and the camera and be grateful for the love that surrounds me. And scrapbooking is what continues to remind me that love is everywhere around me when I stop in the midst of an ordinary moment to notice it among the "small stuff."

Nikki Merson

A Scrapbooker; A Future Mom

One faces the future with one's past.

Pearl S. Buck

Mom, you caught the bouquet at Auntie's wedding?" I asked one day after perusing my gram's old photos.

"Yeah, I think," was her response.

"Why didn't you ever tell me?!" I exclaimed.

"I don't know. I forgot, I guess. Jenn, that was a long time ago," she said in an annoyed tone.

I couldn't believe it—how could she forget? I had recently caught the bouquet at my best friend's wedding, and it had been the highlight of my week. I remember feeling like a star when I caught that bouquet out of all of those pining girls. I was so excited I made a scrapbook page all about it. My own mother, who I struggle sometimes to understand and connect with, had once been a young, single girl who caught the bouquet. Who knew? This experience helped me to grasp a deeper meaning as to why I scrapbook. I always had thought it was merely to find a home for my photos. I was so wrong.

I realize that one day my own life will change through job opportunities, marriage and having children. My kids will know me only as their mom, probably an old, boring mom at that! If it weren't for my scrapbooks, maybe they wouldn't know that I once went white-water rafting, parasailing and skydiving way before they were even a notion. They wouldn't know my dreams, hopes and aspirations for the future. They wouldn't know that, at age twenty-five, I still don't know what I want to be when I grow up. They wouldn't really know me, the whole me, the "me" that was a painfully shy girl, an insecure teenager and now an audacious, young, single woman.

I want my future children and grandchildren to know all of my stories. I want them to be able to identify with me, regardless of how many years we are apart in age. I want to be able to show them that I went through some of the same experiences, hardships and problems that they will inevitably have, and that I understand them because I have actually been there myself. I hope that my scrapbooks will help close the generational gap that sometimes exists between children and parents.

Sometimes I feel sad because it's like there is a whole part to my mom and dad's lives that is a mystery to me. I can't picture them young and carefree. I can't envision what they were like when they were my age. I wonder, how did my dad propose? How did my mom tell the family she was expecting a baby? I wonder, what did they do on dates when they were first married? What were their schedules like when they were young? How did they choose their professions? I wonder so many things. I ask all of these questions, and I get the same answer every time: "Hmmmm, Jenn, I really don't remember."

It baffles me! It frustrates me! It makes me sad! How can they not remember? Then I realize that I, myself, wouldn't be able to remember these little flittering details of life if I hadn't recorded them somehow. So that is why I continue this scrapbook obsession of mine. I approach it as if I am writing letters to my future self (and future children), so that one day I may remember myself as I am now—at age twenty-five, no one's wife yet and no one's mom yet . . . just me, Jenn.

Jennifer Colannino

My Fortune Without a Cookie

The impossible can always be broken down into possibilities.

Author Unknown

Scrapbooking has taught me so much, not only about myself, but about my family. I have learned more about life, the importance of sharing memories with future generations and capturing the daily pieces of living, which makes us who we are.

As I have wandered along my path of development as a scrapbooker, I have faced many roadblocks that I have managed to work through with time and patience. However, one roadblock in my scrapping development seemed to continue to haunt me and hold me back from evolving my talent to its fullest extent.

Through the years, I have created many scrapbook pages, including a wedding album for my husband and me, an adoption album for prospective birth parents, a baby album for our adopted daughter, vacation albums capturing our family escapes, and general albums that encapsulate our daily lives. There is one thing in common in all of my albums: My journaling is 100-percent computer-generated. As any good scrapbooker knows, showcasing your personal handwriting gives meaning and credibility to scrapbook pages. It leaves your personal mark on a page that will extend to future generations, which creates a connection to the person you were. They will actually hold a piece of your existence in their hands and will feel your presence.

I read articles and books and examined other scrapbookers' work to try to get past this roadblock. Each time I attempted my own handwriting on the page, I felt that it ruined the perfect look I had going from an artistic perspective. I just wasn't able to leave my handwriting there, even though that is what all the experts recommend. So I began to hide my hand journaling behind things so I could at least have it on the page, but not visible. I still didn't feel right about this since it was a personal reflection at first glance. I needed to find a way to get past this and was completely out of ideas.

Sometimes the most important life lessons do not come from an expert. I believe that experience and meaning are really our best friends. Little did I know that I was about to have an experience that would move me in the direction of being able to finally place my writing on the page.

I was shopping one day, and my daughter needed socks. So I picked up a few pairs that I found on clearance at a local department store. As always, when I got home I began pulling off tags and stickers. As I opened the very last pair, I found a scribbled message in Chinese characters under the cardboard. Had it been printed by a machine, I would not have given it a second thought, but these

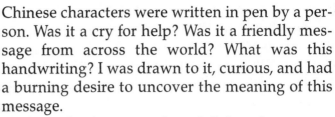

Chinese characters were written in pen by a person. Was it a cry for help? Was it a friendly message from across the world? What was this handwriting? I was drawn to it, curious, and had a burning desire to uncover the meaning of this message.

Through a message board, I found someone who had a Chinese friend and would be more than happy to decode my message. I scanned and sent the Chinese handwriting off for interpretation. I waited on pins and needles for almost two weeks for a response. During my wait, I gave much thought to the message and the person who may be working in that Chinese sock factory. I had created all kinds of interesting possibilities for the interpretation of my special Chinese message. During the second week of waiting, it hit me like a ton of bricks. This message was special, and I was giving it so much thought and time in my life because it was written in someone's penmanship and held real meaning. It wasn't mass-produced; it was an actual message and reflection of a real person! It held important meaning to me, and during that time became a significant part of my life.

Interestingly, when the interpretation came back, the message was advertising the worker's own personal store that was in the town near the factory. It was an invitation of sorts, to be a patron in their own retail establishment. Although this wasn't quite the interpretation I had conjured in my mind of what the mysterious message might hold, it was at this juncture I fully understood the meaning of leaving your penmanship on your pages.

Journaling on scrapbook pages using personal penmanship truly connects future generations to a real person with real meaning who had a real life. When I dug deeper, I understood that it wasn't necessarily the words themselves that held the meaning, but the fact that I held the pen and expressed myself in the way that felt right for me. I leave a real piece of myself on that paper that is forever tied to the person I am and the person I will always be.

Lisa Falduto

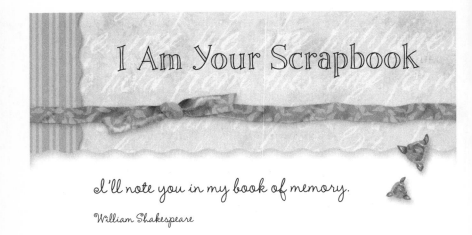

I Am Your Scrapbook

I'll note you in my book of memory.

William Shakespeare

I am special, unique and priceless. I make people smile, laugh, cry and remember. I am quiet, yet speak volumes. I am a work of art and a labor of love. I'm like a member of the family because I share every birthday, holiday, reunion, accomplishment and disappointment. I also share everyday moments and remember secrets you forgot you shared. I am simple, beautiful and ornate. I'll speak for you when you no longer speak. I'll share who you are and what you did with generations to come, just as I introduced you to your ancestors.

I've taught you art when you thought yourself inept. I taught you creativity when you thought yourself unimaginative. You have gained confidence through me. You have made friendships because of me. You have spent countless hours remembering your family and friends, to share them with me in just the right way.

You have changed since our relationship began. You have become more introspective. You have learned to live in the moment. You appreciate your blessings and accept your trials, knowing they all contribute to who you are. You think of me at unlikely moments, roll your eyes and laugh at yourself, knowing it will happen again. You've poured your heart out to me when you weren't ready to share with anyone else. And I've held your secrets until you were ready to share. You give me your treasures and keepsakes, and I give you a glimpse of who you are like no mirror ever could.

Our friendship is endless. I am your scrapbook.

Patricia A. Cable

Buried Treasures

How lucky we are to have such a treasure of memories.

Lady Bird Johnson

In each of our lives, there are the rare moments of indefinable beauty and joy that we will never forget. The scent of a brand-new baby, the feel of soft, smooth baby skin fresh from the womb held against you for the first time and the unforgettable sound of a first cry are memories held so dear to the heart that they will never be far from a mother's thoughts.

There are also the days that feel as if they will never end, the house looks as if a tornado has been through it, the baby is teething and requires your full attention, the phone will not quit ringing, and your head is spinning. The only thing on your side today is that your three-year-old is playing quietly in her room. You check on her only to find that your sweet little girl has become an artist, and her freshly painted walls are her canvas. Scattered across her bedroom wall are fifteen primitive-looking stick men, each adorning one very happy, smiling face. Your little

Picasso looks up at you, green Crayola in one hand, beaming with pride, and through all of the frustration of the day you catch a glimpse of the world she lives in.

I will forever hold my children's stories in my heart, waiting for the perfect moment to be shared. They are one of my most valued treasures; they are irreplaceable and priceless.

Inside of each of us lies these buried treasures waiting to be discovered, looking for a way to come out. Some of us are fortunate enough to have found a way to share these memories in a way that will never be forgotten. I am one of the fortunate. I am a scrapbooker.

To an outsider looking in, I am simply a crafty mother with a roomful of paper, stickers and glue. I have countless albums filled with pictures and writing, and I usually have my camera within arm's reach. To myself I am an author. I capture the stories of my children on film, and I strive to retell them to the best of my ability on the layouts found within their individual scrapbooks.

Over the past six years that I have been creating layouts, scrapbooking has become more than just a hobby to me. It is my creative outlet; I am able to express myself through the pages in my album. It is my journal, capturing my memories, my thoughts and my feelings. It is a time capsule; hidden within the pages of my scrapbooks are countless moments, frozen eternally for us to look back upon. It is my release after a long, stressful day; it is almost like a secret world I can escape to, a world in which I wander through sheets of paper and mounds of embellishments, where color, design and accents are the biggest choices I need to make.

I often joke that these scrapbooks will be a curse to my children; when they are grown adults, they will be burdened with the countless albums that their mother has bestowed upon them. Both their guilt and their loyalty to me will force them to forever hold on to them, finding them a home where they will always be within reach during my visits, but also out of sight the rest of the time. My wish for them is, of course, much greater than a fate like this.

There are times in all of our lives when we wish to reflect, to reminisce. There are times in our lives when we are lonely and need comfort. There are times in our lives when we want nothing more than to hear our mother's voice and feel her unconditional love. My hope is that I am able to offer that support, those words and my love for my children for many years to come. My comfort is that when I am gone, my words, my support and my love will be only a scrapbook away. I hope that when my children open up these albums, they see that they are a labor of love, and when they look through them they will feel their mother's love wrapped around them.

Perhaps one day when my little artist is all grown up, she will look at one of my created layouts, my own canvas. She will picture me with a paper trimmer in one hand beaming with pride, and maybe, just maybe, she'll catch a glimpse of the world through her mother's eyes.

Jennifer Kranenburg

The Single Scrapper

I don't regret for a single moment having lived for pleasure.

Oscar Wilde

Recently in a scrapbooking class I taught, I shared a lot of personal insight about myself and my passion for scrapbooking. Afterward, a rather haughty woman walked up to me, eyebrows raised and a smug smile on her face.

She asked me point-blank, "Why in the world do you scrapbook? It doesn't seem like you have much material without a family."

I knew where the question was coming from, but it still made me wince. *Ouch!* I thought. You see, I'm happily single and child-free at the age of thirty, and during my class, I mentioned this. To most people, I don't fit the profile of a typical scrapbooker. Without children or a husband, I was seemingly a paradox to this woman. She seemed to wonder what memories I could possibly have to scrapbook in my life. In her mind, nothing was worth scrapbooking if it didn't include mass amounts of cootchie-coo babies or romantic weddings. She soon learned (and viewed in my scrapbook) that my life has been one amazing journey in itself; that the everyday moments in my life are just as important as pictures of a baby walking for the first time.

Scrapbooking the single life has shown me how fabulous it is to be a single lady in the new millennium. There are New Year's parties, college parties, homecoming parties (okay, there have been lots of fun parties). There are also my best friends and their weddings that I've proudly stood up in, nights of karaoke and an unforgettable time we all went tubing down the Ausable River. My trips with friends to Chicago, Toronto, Disney World and Las Vegas remind me of my carefree spirit and love of travel. Scenes of each and every trip bring me back to the memories we made on those wonderful days. Every time I flip through the pages, I smile at the time we all posed with bronze statues around the city of Chicago, or the time we all gaped down at the Colorado River from high atop Hoover Dam. I blush when I recall that trip to Las Vegas where . . . well, what happens in Vegas stays in Vegas, right?

Unknown to this haughty lady, being single doesn't mean that nothing happens in my life. In fact, my life has been one scrapbook page after another. In 2001, I literally walked out of a job as a corporate buyer to choose a life of poverty (and complete happiness) as a student in education. After four years of struggling and scrimping, I am now a teacher. In those four years of school, I photographed my first apartment, my fancy SUV—which I traded in for a practical and economical minivan—the buildings around my college campus, my friends and I having TV nights, my mentors that I've encountered along the way and the satisfied feeling of being home, which I experienced the first time I set foot in a classroom as a student teacher. I've preserved what it means to be an educator and the powerful feeling of care and compassion that I hold in my heart for each and every student who enters my classroom. Those are the babies and weddings of my life.

Being single is not an exclusive experience. I'm not the first person ever to be single; I'm just one of the few people who scrapbook about it. I've embraced scrapbooking about those bad dates, bad jobs and all-around bad days I've had as a single woman. They've shown me the character that I've built through each experience. I've learned that my own family, which consists of my parents and my brother, is one fantastic group of people—equally as important as a family I would create for myself. Capturing our special family traditions of miniature golf, traveling to our cottage in northern Michigan, Christmas celebrations and family reunions has taught me the importance of preserving the environment that is unique to me. My world is filled with experiences, the ache of a broken heart and the hurt of losing a job, but also the excitement of new possibilities and endless adventures in my single life.

After the haughty woman put down one of my albums, she looked at me and said, "Well, I still think it would be nice for you to have some family to scrapbook." As she walked away, I shook my head and smiled, realizing that you can't win with some people. But that's okay. I've got too much scrapbooking to do to worry about it.

Maggie Koller

The Blanket

What the heart has once cherished it will never forget.

Author Unknown

When my son, Keith, was born, his grandmother made him a quilted blanket. The blanket was made from a cotton print of a clown holding a bouquet of balloons. The primary colors of the quilt made it very eye-catching. As he was growing up, he would sleep with the blanket, but never seemed to have the need for it. We took the blanket on vacations, but it was used to cover him as he slept in the car. I never noticed any unusual attachment to the blanket, but did notice that it rarely made it to the wash.

When Keith graduated from high school and went off to college, I went into his room at home to clean it and noticed that the blanket was not there. A few days later, I went to see Keith in his dorm room and discovered that he had his blanket with him. In order for others not to find out that he had it, he had placed his blanket in his pillowcase. When I said something to him about it, he said that he liked to feel it on his face when he slept. Deep down, I think it was a piece of home that he could keep with him.

During his freshman year in college, Keith came down with pneumonia and had to come home for a few days. I went to check on him and found him in bed, asleep, hugging his blanket to his face, which was flushed with fever. The sight of him being so sick and clutching his blanket for comfort brought tears to my eyes. Even though he often was quick to remind me that he was grown, he still found comfort in his blanket, which was a piece of his childhood.

Being the scrapbooker that I am, I reached for a camera and took this picture without ever waking him. I searched through some baby pictures and found a picture of him lying on this blanket when he was nine months old. I scrapped a layout using the picture of Keith at nine months as well as the one of him at nineteen. The title of the layout was "The Blanket, Then and Now." Keith still didn't know about the picture or the layout until he came into a scrapbook store that I was teaching in and one of my students said, "Oh, isn't he the one in the blanket layout?" He has since seen the layout and appreciates what I did to document a part of his life. Three years later, he still has the blanket with him at college, and when I visited with him this past weekend, his blanket lay openly on his bed. Inside every grown man is a child needing comfort.

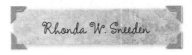

Rhonda W. Sneeden

Can You Hear Me Now?

It is time for parents to teach young people early on that in diversity there is beauty and there is strength.

Maya Angelou

My daughter's audiologist raised an eyebrow when I slyly took out my camera. I know, I know—who would want to remember their child being fitted for hearing aids? Who would want to record on paper with photographic evidence the fact that their child is hearing-impaired? Who would actually create a scrapbook layout with pretty papers and embellishments to enhance sad photos? Wouldn't it be more conventional to take pictures of the birthday parties, the pony rides?

Several reasons made me remove that lens cap. First of all, I wanted to show our daughter, Sophie, how courageous she was when faced with wearing such an awkward and outward sign of her physical limitation. We aren't talking the mini "Miracle Ear" here! These things are bulky

and obvious and interfere with many fashionable hair accessories. Woe is the five-year-old girlie girl! Second, by creating a layout, I am honoring Sophie's differences and hopefully demonstrating to her that we all have our quirks. Hers might be plastic gadgets that improve her hearing, while someone else may have a retainer, glasses or even big feet.

Last, and perhaps the most selfish rationale behind capturing this moment, is my own need to journal about the worries/fears/hopes I have. How do I wrap my brain around this? Sophie has always had challenges to over-come due to Noonan Syndrome, but this is the first noticeable manifestation of her difficulties, a constant, conspicuous reminder that she is, in fact, handicapped. Everything would be different now! Sophie's hearing will markedly improve, yet part of me is sad about how this might affect my little girl. Would people treat her differently? Would she refuse to wear them? Some people might scoff at these questions and criticize me for such worries. These people, however, are usually not the parents of a special-needs child.

In addition to feverishly writing down my feelings regarding Sophie's new wardrobe accessory, I have found that prayer has significantly provided an outlet for coping. Enlisting other church members' prayers reminded me that no detail is too small for God. We were not appealing for a solution to world hunger; nevertheless, the belief that God does care about the minute things in life proves how merciful and gracious he is! And being in his presence jogs my memory about my daughter's gifts. Sophie is blessed beyond measure with a sunny, ethereal glow that attracts people. She laughs and dances at will. She is generally a happy girl. As her mom, I am honored by her strengths and her seeming ability to not care about what others think of her—yet.

Kids can be cruel, and I was going to do my best to educate her peers about Sophie's new "earrings." I asked her kindergarten teacher to read some books about hearing loss in hopes that her classmates would realize her aids were just another part of Sophie. They were not strange or weird, but helpful and innocuous. The children were curious, but once they learned what the hearing aids were, they accepted them and moved on. One of the perks of kids' short attention spans!

Sophie has learned to wear her aids like a pro, and by God's grace she never really had an aversion to them. I pray that her hearing loss does not worsen, and that her future friends learn to embrace the whole of Sophie and not focus on one of her parts. I also hope that one day when she is a young woman, Sophie can reflect on this scrapbook page and feel proud of her fortitude even as an innocent five-year-old girl.

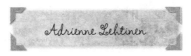

Adrienne Lehtinen

Expecting No. 3

Clever people will recognize and tolerate nothing but cleverness.

Henri Frederic Amiel

After taking two pregnancy tests and realizing that I was in fact pregnant with my third child, I began thinking of ways to tell my husband and family. I had to think of something to top what I had done for the prior two pregnancies.

With our firstborn, I told my husband that I could make it the best day of his life when he came home from a bad day at work. We then told my family by playing "Pictionary," and the puzzle was "Stephanie's Pregnant."

With our second child, I wrapped up the pregnancy test and gave it to my husband on Valentine's Day. For our family and friends we had custom made fortune cookies made that read, "We're having a baby, September 2003."

After racking my brain as to what I could do to announce my third pregnancy, I knew that I could get my creative juices flowing or at least someone else's by posting a message to a local scrapbooking site that I chat on daily.

Although there were several awesome ideas that actually got me thinking, I came up with my own plan. Late one evening after my husband went to bed, I stayed up until 2:00 A.M. (typical scrapbook time for me) and created a scrapbook page that said "Coming Soon, Baby No. 3, December 2005" and had a picture of the pregnancy test on it.

Early the next morning while the kids were in bed and hubby was in the shower, I went downstairs, layout in hand, and started scrubbing the kitchen floor. My husband came down to leave for work. We were chitchatting when I finally said, "Oh, I stayed up late and did this layout for the scrapbook store contest. I want you to look at it and tell me what you think."

He was happy to oblige as he always does when I ask him to observe my hobby. He looked at the page and was very quiet. It seemed like an eternity, but it was probably only a couple of seconds before he turned to me, beaming from ear to ear and smiling with his eyes, and said, "Really!" I said, "Really" and assured him that this was not an April Fools' joke (as it was April 1). We talked for a couple more minutes . . . baby talk, of course. He was excited and giggly. He finally said, "I have to get to work. You got me all emotional." As I said good-bye, I noticed tears in his eyes, and I could feel the joy in his heart. I think I pulled it off again. He even said that he loves the way I tell him the good news in clever ways. Mission accomplished!

Stephanie Menzock

The Kidnapped Bride

Do not the most moving moments of our lives find us without words?

Marcel Marceau

One of the pleasures of scrapbooking is detailing those events that do not fit neatly into those pristine, showy leather albums gracing the coffee table. Take, for example, the traditional wedding album. You have beautiful portraits of the blissful couple, the diffused candlelit shots accenting a newly French-manicured hand and blinding diamond ring, and those endless photos of relatives you see once every five years. Such a collection leaves little room for the funnier, more spontaneous happenings that tell the real story behind the posed smiles. You know, those embarrassing moments comprising the bulk of family reunion gossip? I believe such instances deserve a prominent place in our archives because these are the juicy parts of our history that our children's children will relish!

I have embarked on creating such a legacy. My own wedding was filled with unconventional occurrences amid the froufrou bridal dress and church service. The special day was scheduled to be traditional in a Norman Rockwell kind of way. Of course, we all know what happens when we plan the "perfect" day—expect the unexpected! Well, who knew a kidnapping was on the menu sandwiched between the filet mignon and ceremonial cake?

The fact that I was marrying a mischievous man should have been the flashing red-light warning of things to come. Couple that with my fiancé importing one of his Finnish matrimonial traditions (unbeknownst to me), and it made for a very interesting gathering indeed. Sure, I'd been to two Finnish weddings, and at one of them it did happen, but never in a million years did I think, on *my* wedding day, at *my* reception, I would be kidnapped by rambunctious, rowdy pirates (namely our brothers and their Finnish accomplices). They lifted me up, 400-pound dress and all, threw one of my dainty size ten heels to the guests (who wondered if they should call 911), and carried me out of the party. Down the street we went: me, helpless maiden (well, now matron) being hoisted several feet off the ground by five beefy bandits. They tugged on my veil and snorted and heckled—very jolly, but striding steadfastly toward their destination: the local Rusty Hammer tavern.

By Finnish tradition, the bride is stolen during the reception and held for ransom (usually at a nearby watering hole where the pirates raise their pints to a job well done). Once my shock subsided, I embraced the merriment and giggled when I remembered the looks on my fellow countrymen's faces; we Americans never saw *this* coming! Before departing the pub, I was relieved to see that these incorrigible villains at least paid the tab. Outside I realized I was a one-shoed, helpless damsel unable to walk back to the soiree, not that it mattered since I was heaved above their heads and carried in a style reminiscent of mosh pits at rock concerts. I uncontrollably laughed until I cried (and then shrieked when they crossed the street against the light and actually stopped traffic). I can only imagine what those drivers thought as a poof of silk satin floated by on the shoulders of men with eye patches.

Back at the party, my new husband was in the middle of reciting ten reasons why he wanted me back. A few notable ones included: the honeymoon was paid for, because he loved me, because he loved me (said in Finnish), and because I was so darn beautiful! Afterward, my shoe resurfaced, brimming with ransom money collected from the guests. At the end of the evening, I happily recounted the kidnapping caper, wanting to savor each aspect of this escapade. I was thrilled that my more commonplace agenda was abandoned in favor of an improvised one; I could not have written the script for a better day!

This is one story that is remembered fondly by friends and family, one story that may have remained undocumented had I not tucked it away in my scrapbook. There really isn't a place for journaling about the festive, amusing anecdotes of one's wedding in those gorgeous, professional albums. It is my hope that my children will be able to relive the love and gaiety of our union, not just through our elegant photos, but also via the tales behind the photos.

Adrienne Lehtinen

The Road Less Traveled

At first dreams seem impossible, then improbable, then inevitable.

Christopher Reeve

My husband has always told me that I am a dreamer. I dream about where I want to go, what I want to do in life and how I can make life better for myself and my family. Some people dream about things all of their lives and never do anything to make their dreams come true. After spending seventeen years working as a registered nurse, I decided it was time for me to pursue some of my dreams. Terrified, excited and anxious, I approached my husband with the idea of opening a scrapbook store. To my surprise, he agreed. Together we set out on the road less traveled and opened the first scrapbooking store on Long Island.

I put my whole self into my entrepreneurship. I researched products, ordered supplies, designed the store layout and soon opened the doors to eager scrapbookers.

Women came from all over. Day after day, week after week, people came into the shop and talked about themselves and their loved ones. Soon I felt that I had become a part of their families, too. My store and I were welcomed by these wonderful scrappers with open arms.

As I met more and more people each day, the excitement grew and so did the ideas. There were so many ideas in my head on which classes to teach, which layouts to display, which new products to order and what this industry was missing. As a newfound scrapbooking friend and I got to know each other better, we found out that we had another craft in common—quilling. At the time, there was no quilling in scrapbooking. So we put our minds and dollars together and wrote a book about quilling in scrapbooks. Not too long after that, I collaborated with another company to write my second idea book on quilling in scrapbooks. I had no idea of the journey I was about to embark on . . . I had just knocked on the door of opportunity, and it had opened wide!

With a lot of elation, hard work and dedication, soon I was teaching at different consumer and retail trade shows around the country, meeting many exuberant scrappers. I flew to Tennessee a few times to be a guest on the *DIY Scrapbooking* TV show—how exciting that was to teach millions of viewers techniques in scrapbooking! And before I knew it, I was designing my own product line with Creative Imaginations. "Superbusy" became my middle name! Still owning my scrapbook store, more opportunities kept coming, and I could not say no! I had to pinch myself often to see if it was all real!

Now I feel my journey is far from over. I have so much more to accomplish, so much more I want to learn and so much more I want to teach, but I take it one day at a time. Looking back on my passage and following the footsteps backward in my mind, it seems like an illusion. I sometimes wonder, *How did I arrive here? How did I get this far?* And then I think, *ah yes, it was following a dream and choosing the road less traveled.*

My Faraway Love

If I had never met him, I would have dreamed him into being.

Anzia Yezierska

Even though I am a hopeless romantic, I could never have imagined fourteen years ago as I sat in front of the computer that I would type some words that would change my life forever. The historic subject line that seems so plain when looking back was but a window into my forever: "Nice to meet you." I could not have dreamed that on the other end of the world, ten thousand miles away, sat a man at a computer who was destined to be my faraway love.

I have heard it said there are dozens of matches out in the world that a person could potentially marry. And it is believed that only timing and circumstances decide upon the winning marriage union. I can accept that there are many mates that could probably result in a fairly good marriage, but the romantic side of my heart truly believes there is one very special person in that large potential group that is your true soul mate.

And so, with absolutely no thoughts of love or destiny or soul mates, I decided to start a pen-pal friendship. I stared blankly at hundreds of newsgroup postings for pen pals. The first one I tried to reply to was immediately bounced back. I almost assumed I was doing something wrong and packed up my books to go, when a subject line from New Zealand grabbed my attention. Yes, I would like to have a pen pal to write to from New York to New Zealand.

We must have known that we were meant for each other even before either of us would be brave enough to admit it, as we both saved every single piece of e-mail, snail mail, postcards and letters that ever arrived. After two years of writing to each other, we noticed the change in our letters. The phrases "take care" and "sincerely yours" changed to "always thinking of you" and eventually "forever yours." Our letters were incredibly flirtatious. Often we tempted each other on paper with wonderfully romantic ideas like sitting together by a crackling fireplace sipping cocoa and snuggling under a blanket. However, we both agreed that due to the distance, we would always just be happy keeping it a written relationship.

Ken came to the United States for a business trip in 1993, and I ultimately found out that I was the real business he had to sort out. We had only ten days together, but we packed a lot into those days—pancakes at the local diner, hikes and sitting in the gardens, and visits to a nearby lake. Everywhere we went, we were falling more and more in love, but both of us agreed that we could not be in love with each other. Even when he pulled me close and kissed me, my heart was saying I never wanted his kisses to end, but my head was saying, "He goes away in just a few days."

The last afternoon we spent together, we decided that we should continue our romantic letters. We would see other people in our respective countries and go on with our lives, but always have each other on the other side of the world. In our last hours together, though, Ken leaned over and stared at me after a long silence. He had been deep in thought, and he quietly announced, "But I don't want to see other people, and I don't want you to either." I was so full of joy that I embraced him, and we knew that we could make it happen. It would be hard, but our love was strong because we fell in love before we even met! That's pure fairy-tale love . . . the kind that lasts a lifetime.

When Ken left on the plane back to New Zealand, we made a plan that I would save up my money and make a visit to see him in New Zealand about ten months later. That seemed like an eternity to a young girl in love, so this is when I decided that I needed to find a concrete way to preserve every little detail of the memories from our time together.

Scrapbooking provided me with the strength to make it through the long months when I was feeling sad and lonely. I took all the photos of our days together and created lovely scrapbook memories, journaling all the fine little details of what we ate or quotes of what we discussed or what I was dreaming about while I listened to his sexy accent. At times, tears dripped down on the pages because I was missing him so much.

There was the page with the first photo taken of us together, which was centered in between pictures of my college campus. One page featured all the funny little things I love about Ken in person, the kinds of things that don't come across through mail. I had devoted many hours to carefully create a memorable vision of each of our days together. Through the lonely winter nights, I could see the days we spent together and dream of those moments until we could be reunited in New Zealand.

When I finally made it to New Zealand, it was a short ten-day visit once again. I was shocked on my first night when Ken blurted out, "I can't do this distance dating anymore. We need to break it off (my heart crushed in a split second)—or should we get married?" (Yeah, my heart rejoiced)! I got the official fairy-tale proposal with the ring on the beach under the full moonlit sky.

Reality set in when we realized that I had to finish my master's degree, and Ken had to prepare for the big move to America and marriage! And so, history repeats itself—we decided that we would have to be apart again for another eleven months until we could become husband and wife. By now I had learned the strength of comfort that came from my first scrapbook, so I took tons of photos and started this memory book right in New Zealand so I could gather brochures from the places we visited and have Ken help me create the stories on each page. This made our journey especially nice because we were capturing the memories and the spirit of the romance with each page of our scrapbook. The idea that someday we would be showing this book to our children when they asked about how Mommy and Daddy met and fell in love made my heart smile.

We are celebrating our ten-year wedding anniversary this week with our three-year-old son,

Rylin, and one-year-old daughter, Karyna Rose. I keep up my very detailed scrapbooks of our life as a family. I know how powerful a photo can be when you are missing someone. So when the kids eventually go away to college and leave us feeling sad and lonely, we can snuggle up under a blanket by the fire, drink our cocoa and look through our scrapbooks. We will reminisce about all the places we have been together and share stories of the children's adventures while we once again spend time waiting . . . for scrapbooks of grandchildren!

Larae Mary Fowler

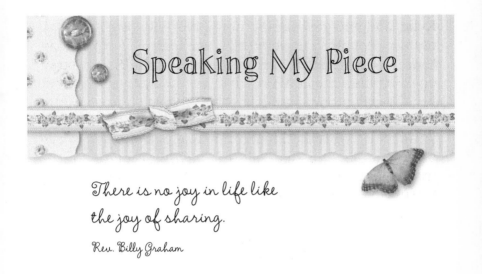

Speaking My Piece

*There is no joy in life like
the joy of sharing.*

Rev. Billy Graham

"... the creator of the award-winning Web site ... Please welcome . . . Angie Pedersen!" The words floated back to me behind the soundstage, and I was struck by the magnitude of the moment. My heart fluttered, and my breath caught. *What was I doing here? How could I go out there and speak to nearly two thousand people? Would they notice if I just turned around and left?*

Rewind three months to March 2003. My first book had been out for just under a year. I received an e-mail from an event planner for Close to My Heart, a direct-sales scrapbooking and stamping company. She inquired about my availability as a guest speaker for their annual convention in June. *Me? A keynote speaker?* My skin tingled as I told my husband about the opportunity. With his enthusiastic support, I proudly agreed to speak at the convention.

Over the next couple of months, I finalized details for my presentation on the importance of scrapbooking about oneself. My friends were so excited for me; I was amazed at the outpouring of support I received in my preparations. Several kind consultants mentored me as I stamped my layout examples. My son guided me as I put together my PowerPoint presentation. My publisher gave me tips on speaking in front of large audiences.

I flew to Portland, Oregon, the day before my speech. Later that evening, I placed a phone call to my husband back home. We chatted about my flight and the kids. He asked me if I was nervous. Suddenly overwhelmed by insecurity and self-doubt, I dissolved into tears. I was sure I would forget everything I wanted to say, the audience would be bored, and the event planners would be disappointed they chose me. My husband was sympathetic and gently reassured me. "Those event planners know what they're doing," he pointed out. "They asked you because you're who you are. Your ideas are worth sharing, Angie," he reminded me. "You're there for a reason. You just have to live up to it."

The morning of the presentation, I woke up at 5:10 A.M., proof of the adrenaline already pumping through my system. At 7:30 A.M. I entered the room where the keynote would be held. It was enormous! Rows and rows of chairs, lights streaming across the stage, rock music already blaring—I soon realized why the event required a separate production company. It was like a big rock concert! I went backstage and they "mike'd" me: a little receiver box hooked to my waistband, a wire over my ear and a little wire rounded in front of my mouth for the microphone. With about an hour left until my speech, I went backstage to look over my notes and compose myself. I found myself quickly engrossed in all the behind-the-scenes activity, however. The soundboard area was a complex arrangement of computers, wires, monitors, buttons, knobs and a crew of six technicians. Far above my head was a mammoth hydraulic lift, necessary for reaching more wires and equipment. I could see the two huge screens on either side of the stage, lit from behind with bright colors, and two sets of stairs, leading to "stage left" and "stage right." The enormity of what I was about to do started to sink in.

The time remaining flew by, and it was my turn to speak. It was something, standing backstage, waiting to go up those stairs, listening to them introduce me. There was a slight buzzing in my ears, and I felt a little light-headed. It seemed like time stood still for just the briefest moment, and I thought to myself, *This is really it. I'm going to speak to nearly two thousand people, and it's just me.* It was such a humbling, yet empowering moment. I truly think I will remember that moment for the rest of my life, my heart thudding in my chest, just before I went up the stairs to go out onstage. I'm so glad I took a picture of my view from backstage; that's just the moment I want to scrap.

The audience clapped and cheered as I walked out. I felt like a "deer in the headlights," faced with hundreds of people watching me, but I promptly shook it off. I thought of all the people who supported me in my preparations, and it was like they were there with me, cheering me on. I took comfort in their strength. Breathing deep, I started speaking my piece.

"Your stories are unique," I told them. "You've lived a life worth remembering. Your stories are worth telling," I encouraged them. "Let me ask you this: If you don't tell your stories, who will?" By the audience's slightly stunned expressions, I could tell I'd made my point.

The presentation went very smoothly—everyone laughed when they were supposed to and nodded in approval when my words struck a chord. The forty-five minutes flew by, and then I was done.

Backstage they "de-miked" me, and I gathered my wits and my things. Afterward, I signed books for about two and a half hours before the crowd started to thin out. I was completely overwhelmed by the response. In that time, I heard such moving stories from audience members. One woman said she had to step out during my presentation because my points really hit home for her. Another woman told me she bought my book for her sister, who struggles with depression. Another woman thanked me for convincing her she's a part of her family, and that her stories are worth scrapbooking.

After that convention, I realized what it means to "make it" in the scrapbooking industry. For me, it means I have opportunities to share my ideas with people from all walks of life. It means that my words have found a home with people who need them. It means that those people, in turn, share themselves with me, through their personal, intimate stories. I have witnessed the power of personal stories, and that has been a blessing.

Angie Pedersen

Scrapbooker's Dictionary

ARCHIVAL SAFE: A locked container for scrapbook supplies.

CHOCOLATE: Food for thought.

CRAFTY: What a woman should be in order to hide scrapbook purchases from her husband.

CREATIVE JUICES: Beverages consumed while scrapbooking.

CROP: (verb) To remove all the dirty dishes, piles of clothes and other household clutter from photos. (noun) A get-together where scrapbookers eat, drink, socialize and occasionally complete a page layout.

DIE CUT: A scrapbooking injury caused by a craft knife, scissors or other sharp object.

ENLARGEMENT: What needs to be done to every scrapbooker's workspace.

HOMEMADE: What every scrapbooker needs so they can spend more time scrapbooking and less time cleaning.

LAYOUT: What photos, papers and embellishments do on a scrapbooker's table for hours (sometimes days) at a time.

PAGE PROTECTOR: A scrapbooker with young children.

PAPER PUNCH: What a scrapbooker does when she realizes the paper she is using is not true 12 x 12 inches. (See Twelve By Twelve.)

PHOTO OPPORTUNITY: A sale at a camera store.

PRECIOUS MOMENTS: Time spent scrapbooking.

REPRINTS: What's left behind after little fingers touch your photos over and over again.

SCRAPBOOK RETREAT: When you walk away from a scrapbook layout in progress for a period of time so as to better evaluate it upon returning.

SCRAPBOOK STORE: What you do with the album you bought just because it looked so cute.

SPRAY ADHESIVE: What a scrapbooker should do when she finds a good man who supports her hobby.

TRIMMER: What a scrapbooking hobby makes your wallet.

TWELVE BY TWELVE (12 X 12) INCHES: Size of paper that is anywhere from 11¾" x 11¾" to 12¼" x 12¼", but rarely 12" x 12".

UN-DU: An imaginary button you wish you could press when you make a mistake on a scrapbook layout.

Heather Dewaelsche

Not Another Doll

When we give cheerfully and accept gratefully, everyone is blessed.

Maya Angelou

My four-year-old daughter, Sage, and her friends were giggling, and after hearing them laugh nonstop for several minutes, I headed to the toy room to see what was so funny. What I saw didn't make me laugh—instead, I was quite upset. The girls had dragged my beloved doll head from storage, were spraying strange concoctions in her hair and then combing it in obscure ways. I was shocked. "Don't you know how special this is to Mommy?" I proclaimed. Sage stared at me as if I'd lost it emotionally. How could Mom act so strange over a doll head?

I realized how silly I was being and calmly put the head—hair still a mess—back in its place. Then it dawned on me. How could Sage or anyone else know the significance of the doll head unless I communicated why it was valuable to me? Within a week, I'd created a scrapbook page so my family and future generations would know the story of the doll head and its impact on me.

When I was ten, I spent weeks before Christmas poring through a Sears catalog, marking all the presents I wanted Santa to bring. Since I loved playing with hair, at the top of my list was a doll head complete with a comb, brush and other accessories. The catalog showed two dolls—one that was very beautiful and one that was very homely. I kept showing my mom the picture and telling her, "I want the pretty doll, not the ugly one." I could hardly wait for Christmas morning—I knew I was getting the beautiful doll head.

Imagine my shock and horror when I opened my gift and discovered the ugly doll head. I threw a big fit and ran to my room sobbing. I spent a good share of the day there—crying my eyes out, yet embarrassed at how I was acting. I couldn't understand how my mom had gotten everything so mixed up.

Later that night, I finally rejoined the family, only to find my mom with red, swollen eyes, too. She'd cried as much as I had. I looked at my weary mom and thought of all the things she'd had to do to get ready for Christmas—cook meals, clean house, decorate the tree, make goodies for neighbors, bake gingerbread houses, put up lights, shovel snow, send cards and letters, wrap presents, host parties and, last but not least, buy exactly the right present for a snobby ten-year-old girl.

I suddenly knew I'd been ungrateful and vowed to keep that doll head for the rest of my life. It serves as a reminder to be appreciative for everything received in life—no matter how big, how small, how beautiful or even how homely. This was not another doll.

Lisa Bearnson

The Write Stuff

Your own journal awaits you. Jump.

SARK

F or as long as I can remember, I've always enjoyed reading and writing. In grade school, when my friends dreaded doing book reports and other writing assignments, I relished them. In high school, English and literary classes were my favorites. In college, I preferred essay exams over other types of tests, so it was no surprise that I earned a degree in journalism.

They say a picture is worth a thousand words, but to me, words are priceless. That doesn't mean I don't value photographs . . . quite the contrary, in fact. Ask anyone who knows me, and they will tell you what a picture person I am. (Actually, they will probably call me insane about capturing moments on film!) I am always the one, without fail, who brings a camera to every event. Every birthday party, every holiday, every trip to the park, every visit to the museum, every time I think my kids just look cute, I'm there with my camera. I love taking pictures, and I love looking at them.

But if I had to choose between receiving a boxful of my great-grandmother's photos or a boxful of her journals, the journals would win, hands down. Why? Because although the photos would be fun to look at, they would only leave me with more questions—questions that would forever go unanswered. Questions like, "Who is that girl standing next to her?" or "What was she thinking at that moment?" or even "What was her life like?" I would certainly cherish photos of my great-grandmother, but I would cherish her journals—her words—even more. Through her words, I would come to know the great-grandmother I never met. I would discover more about the woman my mom loved so much. I would learn about her thoughts, her feelings, her hopes, her dreams, her fears, her loves, her life. I am sad to say that my great-grandmother did not leave behind any journals for me to read. But my great-grandchildren will not be able to say the same about me. One day they will have my scrapbooks, filled not only with pictures to look at, but also words—my words—to read.

Even more important to me than leaving a legacy for future generations, though, is making sure my children know exactly how I feel about them—how much they are cherished and loved. Sure, I tell my children I love them— usually several times a day! But just in case there is a day when I forget to tell them, or I am unable to tell them—or, God forbid, I am no longer here to tell them—they will know that they are loved, because it is right there in black and white.

And the words I have written say so much more than just "I love you." They will tell my son, Peyton, how, when he was six months old, his father and I cried softly as we watched his tiny body strapped down for an MRI scan— how horribly gripping our fear was . . . and the wonderful relief we felt upon hearing he was all right. They will tell my daughter, Lindsey, that for the first four months of her

life, she only slept at night when I held her on my chest—
and that I broke down in tears when I was helpless to console her as a colicky infant. My children will know that I
stayed up until four o'clock in the morning making preparations for their first birthday parties. And despite the fact
that their birthdays are both within weeks of Christmas, I
have vowed to always try to make them special.

I used to dream of writing a best-selling novel. Now I
realize that I am the author of the most important story
ever written—at least, to my family. It is the story of our
lives. From the special events to the mundane, my scrapbook pages chronicle everything that is wonderful, heart-
warming, frustrating, crazy and unique about my children
and our family. No, it's not a best-selling novel—it is so
much more. It is a gift to my children—it is my memories,
my thoughts, my feelings, my words . . . it is my heart and
soul. And no one can put a price on that.

Heather Dewaelsche

You're Never Too Late

At seventy-eight, I am really set in my ways
And I know how I want to spend my days.
Doing artwork and yard work
All of which I never shirk.
Then my wife says, "When are you going
to do something with your old navy pics?"
I say, "Maybe sometime when I have
watched all the DVD flicks."
Now what does she do, but get me an album with
the Navy emblem on the front? What to do?
I begin the life of a scrapbooker
With lots of paper to make my album a looker.
They are all in one neat place
With memories that time can't erase.
And as for me, I've saved all kinds of face
As I have become a scrapbooker.

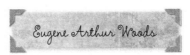

Eugene Arthur Woods

Reprinted by permission of Mack Dobbie ©2005.

Never Again

A gift is pure when it is given from the heart to the right person at the right time and at the right place, and when we expect nothing in return.

Bhagavad Gita

It was 7:00 A.M. on Mother's Day morning when I pushed wearily away from my desk, slipped the last of two dozen scrapbook pages into their clear plastic covers and vowed to never, ever scrapbook again.

It had seemed like such a nice, pleasant, simple idea at first, to make my mom this keepsake for Mother's Day. The gift was the perfect combination of thoughtful and relatively inexpensive, ideal for a near-destitute college student. True, I had never actually tried my hand at scrapbooking before, yet I had seen it done on television many times. *That looks easy enough*, I'd said to myself. *I could turn out one of those babies in no time.*

If only I had realized the amount of time, care and effort

that went into creating each and every scrapbook page, I never would have waited until the day before Mother's Day to begin the project. Yet I had waited, and now I was paying the price.

I had worked clear through the night, digging into boxes of old photographs, carefully selecting and cropping pictures of myself and my three brothers, laying out pages and choosing just the right embellishments to accent the photos. Now the floor of my room was littered with tiny scraps of colored paper, and visions of acid-free stickers swam before my bleary eyes. The book was finished, yet I never wanted to see another heart-shaped hole punch, star-shaped die cut or pair of decorative scissors again as long as I lived.

With tired hands still tacky from glue sticks, I wrapped my mother's scrapbook in tissue paper and headed off to meet my family for breakfast. *First thing I do when I get back,* I vowed, *is light a big fire and watch those scrapbooking supplies burn!* After all, I wouldn't be in need of them again.

Breakfast with my family was wonderful. It was great to be together again—my mom, my three brothers and me. We relived old stories, teased one another and laughed until the waitresses began looking at us like we had just fallen out of the cuckoo's nest. Finally, the time came to give my mother her present. Stifling a tired yawn, I handed over the sloppily wrapped gift and watched as she pulled away the tissue paper in that slow, "it looks too pretty to unwrap" way that mothers have. It wasn't until I heard Mom's excited gasp of joy, however, that I woke up completely for the first time all morning.

The next thing I knew, my brothers were also gathered around the book, flipping through pages, pointing and exclaiming over pictures they never knew existed. There

were photographs of my
older brother Tony as a
newborn coming home from
the hospital and pictures of
the two of us learning to ride
bikes. There was the picture of
my brother Matthew as a baby,
red-faced and struggling in my eight-
year-old arms. I stared up at the camera
with a look that clearly begged, "Please get
this thing off my lap!" There were pictures of
our youngest brother Timothy at fourteen months
old, gleefully romping around the house despite his broken and bandaged left hand, the result of an injury from
which he still sported a scar.

As the pages turned, we watched our personalities
develop through the photographs. There were pictures of
Tony in front of his computer, me wrestling with the family
dog, Matthew with his sunglasses and backward baseball
cap and Timothy with his soccer ball. And in the midst of
it all was our mother, rocking babies, throwing birthday
parties and stitching the stuffing back into torn teddy
bears. It was all there, the joyful moments of our lives
together summed up within the pages of a scrapbook.

Only then did it truly hit me, as the five of us gathered
around the book. This was what it was all about. This was
the reason for making a scrapbook. It wasn't about the
fancy papers, the shiny stickers or the rubber stamps. It
wasn't about spending hours on the perfect layout, creating themes for each page with just the right color scheme.
Yet I had been so concerned with all those trivial things
that I had turned the process into a chore, rather than the
act of love it was meant to be.

Now, as I pored over the scrapbook with my family, I saw it for what it truly was. It was a book of memories, a book that showcased the history of my family and the love we have for one another. It was a book with the power to draw us closer together, and for the first time all morning, I was happy to have created it.

Never scrapbook again? I asked myself. Well ... maybe next year!

Christina Dotson

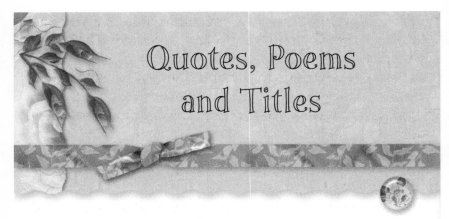

In my writing I am acting as a mapmaker, an explorer of psychic areas . . . a cosmonaut of inner space. . . .

William Burroughs

You've read some very inspiring stories. Some have made you laugh. Some have made you cry. Some have made you think. And many have created a lasting memory. Now it's time to create some lasting memories of your own.

Your recollections, your thoughts, your words—they are an incredible legacy, *your* incredible legacy.

Sounds pretty daunting, doesn't it? It's not. The journaling for your scrapbook pages is right inside you. You only need to let it out. It's the thoughts that run through your head when you're alone at night. It's the memory from the night before that brings a smile to your face the next morning. It's the stuff you never want to forget. It's the good stuff.

When you look at your photographs, take a moment to close your eyes and just think. That woman who is in the photograph—what are your memories of her? If you had to picture her in an outfit, which one would it be? How would she wear her hair?

Use all of your senses. What did she look like? What colors did she favor? What fragrance do you associate with her? Was it a heady, rich perfume, or was it the sweet smell of baking cookies?

What about sounds? How did she talk? Was it with a funny accent? Did she sing? Did she always have music playing in the background?

And then there's the sense of touch. When she pulled you in to hug you, was she strong? Did her shoulders and arms make you feel as though she would always protect you? Or did you feel as though you needed to protect her because of her frail embrace?

If she stood beside you now, how would you feel? Would you stand taller? Would you stand in awe?

Ask yourself simple questions. Then dig deeper. Why would you stand taller next to her? Is it because she inspired you to do things you feared? Or is it because you knew you made her proud? Do the memories of the crisp linen blazers she wore to church every Sunday influence you to choose linen drapes for your home? If you had to think of a dozen little habits of hers, what would they be?

Jot it all down. Jot everything down. Even if the writing isn't perfect, you're capturing memories ... memories that we all know fade too fast. So close your eyes now and use all your senses to gather those special memories and preserve them for generations to come. You will be glad you did.

Jennifer Howland

More Chicken Soup?

Many of the stories and poems you have read in this book were submitted by readers like you who had read earlier *Chicken Soup for the Soul* books. We publish many *Chicken Soup for the Soul* books every year. We invite you to contribute a story to one of these future volumes.

Stories may be up to twelve-hundred words and must uplift or inspire. You may submit an original piece, something you have read or your favorite quotation on your refrigerator door.

To obtain a copy of our submission guidelines and a listing of upcoming *Chicken Soup* books, please write, fax or check our Web site.

Please send your submissions to: *www.chickensoup.com* or mail to:

Chicken Soup for the Soul
P.O. Box 30880, Santa Barbara, CA 93130
fax: 805-563-2945

We will be sure that both you and the author are credited for your submission.

For information about speaking engagements, other books, audiotapes, workshops and training programs, please contact any of our authors directly.

The Leeza Gibbons Memory Foundation

Founded in 2002 by Leeza Gibbons and her family, the Leeza Gibbons Memory Foundation has been created in tribute to Leeza's mother and grandmother, and in response to the growing needs of both those who suffer from memory disorders and their caregivers.

By blending best practices from contemporary social services, health care and advocacy efforts, we are creating a national community of physicians, local nonprofits, individuals, caregivers, universities and researchers dedicated to community, care and a cure for Alzheimer's disease and related memory disorders.

Leeza's Place and the "Memory Consortium"

At the epicenter is the establishment of Leeza's Places across the country. With Leeza's Place serving as the hub, the Foundation seeks to establish a community "memory consortium" comprised of support, research, a continuum of care, political advocacy, acceptance and wellness. The Foundation is committed to ensuring that no person feels unsupported, alone or lost when a diagnosis is made, while simultaneously advocating for better standards of care, treatment and research.

Leeza's Place serves as an "oasis" for education, empowerment and energy for caregivers and their recently diagnosed loved ones, and is managed day to day by the Leeza Care Advocate. Through the establishment of its community-centered Leeza's Places, the Foundation is developing a vital and long overdue supportive presence:

- Creating an intergenerational approach to intervention that will educate, empower and energize every caregiver, concerned relative and diagnosed individual
- Developing memory consortiums in every county, in every state across the country
- Developing continuums of care in communities nationwide
- Collaborating with universities and agencies that promote care, treatment and research
- Advocating and promoting early detection and identification programs of all memory disorders
- Developing affiliations with memory centers, agencies and the neurological community driving research and behavioral outcomes
- Supporting clinical trials and advocacy programs that promote research and curative strategies
- Advocating for key legislative issues at the county, state and national levels

With the growth of Leeza's Places and the corresponding development of their community "memory consortiums," the Foundation is quickly creating a national community where research is collected, information shared, and most importantly, people realize that there is hope for the future.

Hope arouses, as nothing else can arouse, a passion for the possible.

William Sloane Coffin, Jr.

Who Is Jack Canfield?

Jack Canfield is the co-creator and editor of the *Chicken Soup for the Soul*® series, which *Time* magazine has called "the publishing phenomenon of the decade." The series now has 105 titles with over 100 million copies in print in forty-one languages. Jack is also the co-author of eight other bestselling books including *The Success Principles™: How to Get from Where You Are to Where You Want to Be, Dare to Win, The Aladdin Factor, You've Got to Read This Book, The Power of Focus: How to Hit Your Business, Personal and Financial Targets with Absolute Certainty.*

Jack has recently developed a telephone coaching program and an online coaching program based on his most recent book *The Success Principles.* He also offers a seven-day Breakthrough to Success seminar every summer, which attracts 400 people from fifteen countries around the world.

Jack is the CEO of Chicken Soup for the Soul Enterprises and the Canfield Training Group in Santa Barbara, California, and Founder of the Foundation for Self-Esteem in Culver City, California. He has conducted intensive personal and professional development seminars on the principles of success for over 900,000 people in twenty-one countries around the world. He has spoken to hundreds of thousands of others at numerous conferences and conventions and has been seen by millions of viewers on national television shows such as *The Today Show, Fox and Friends, Inside Edition, Hard Copy,* CNN's *Talk Back Live, 20/20, Eye to Eye,* and the *NBC Nightly News* and the *CBS Evening News.*

Jack is the recipient of many awards and honors, including three honorary doctorates and a Guinness World Records Certificate for having seven *Chicken Soup for the Soul* books appearing on the *New York Times* bestseller list on May 24, 1998.

To write to Jack or for inquiries about Jack as a speaker, his coaching programs or his seminars, use the following contact information:

Jack Canfield
The Canfield Companies
P.O. Box 30880
Santa Barbara, CA 93130
Phone: 805-563-2935 • Fax: 805-563-2945
E-mail: *info@jackcanfield.com*
Web site: *www.jackcanfield.com*

Who Is Mark Victor Hansen?

In the area of human potential, no one is more respected than Mark Victor Hansen. For more than thirty years, Mark has focused solely on helping people from all walks of life reshape their personal vision of what's possible. His powerful messages of possibility, opportunity and action have created powerful change in thousands of organizations and millions of individuals worldwide.

He is a sought-after keynote speaker, bestselling author and marketing maven. Mark's credentials include a lifetime of entrepreneurial success and an extensive academic background. He is a prolific writer with many bestselling books, such as *The One Minute Millionaire, The Power of Focus, The Aladdin Factor* and *Dare to Win,* in addition to the *Chicken Soup for the Soul* series. Mark has made a profound influence through his library of audios, videos and articles in the areas of big thinking, sales achievement, wealth building, publishing success, and personal and professional development.

Mark is the founder of the MEGA Seminar Series. MEGA Book Marketing University and Building Your MEGA Speaking Empire are annual conferences where Mark coaches and teaches new and aspiring authors, speakers and experts on building lucrative publishing and speaking careers. Other MEGA events include MEGA Marketing Magic and My MEGA Life.

He has appeared on television (*Oprah,* CNN and *The Today Show*), in print (*Time, U.S. News & World Report, USA Today, New York Times* and *Entrepreneur*) and on countless radio interviews, assuring our planet's people that "you can easily create the life you deserve."

As a philanthropist and humanitarian, Mark works tirelessly for organizations such as Habitat for Humanity, American Red Cross, March of Dimes, Childhelp USA and many others. He is the recipient of numerous awards that honor his entrepreneurial spirit, philanthropic heart and business acumen. He is a lifetime member of the Horatio Alger Association of Distinguished Americans, an organization that honored Mark with the prestigious Horatio Alger Award for his extraordinary life achievements.

Mark Victor Hansen is an enthusiastic crusader of what's possible and is driven to make the world a better place.

Mark Victor Hansen & Associates, Inc.
P.O. Box 7665
Newport Beach, CA 92658
phone: 949-764-2640 • fax: 949-722-6912
Web site: *www.markvictorhansen.com*

Who Is Allison Connors?

Due to her mother's influence, Allison has been involved with crafts all of her life. She also developed a love of creative writing in high school—with poems and stories published in the school's annual publication. Scrapbooking helped Allison put these two skills together . . . and for her, that was the beginning of an interesting turn in her life.

After working as a registered nurse for seventeen years, Allison decided she needed something different. So in July 1999, along with her husband, Tom, they opened the first scrapbook store on Long Island, New York (Scrapbook Alley Ltd.). Together they worked for five years bringing the love and art of scrapbooking to the New York community and finally closing their retail doors in August 2004, only to find themselves branching out in other ways within the scrapbooking world.

Since opening and closing the scrapbook store, Allison has written two books about quilling in scrapbooks. *Creative Quilling for Scrapbooks* (co-authored with Patricia Nelson), and the second book *Twist It, Twirl It, Tie It, Curl It*. Allison has taught at various consumer shows, CKU's and at scrapbook stores around the country. She has also appeared on *DIY Scrapbooking* and on CBS's *The Early Show*.

In the fall of 2003, Allison's product line Quilling Quirks debuted with Creative Imaginations at Memory Trends. Soon after Memory Trends 2003, Allison became the editor of *Scrapbooking.com* magazine as well as a designer for the same publication.

In February 2005, Allison's product line with Creative Imaginations took on her own name: allison connors. Her line of 3-D embellishments continues to grow with every trade show and can be found in countless scrapbooking and craft stores around the country. Allison has served on two design teams—Janlynn and Little Black Dress Designs. Her design work appears at trade shows, on packaging and in publications.

Allison continues to teach scrapbooking, but also wanted to reach out to help people again. So after a brief hiatus, she is working as a registered nurse. She spends three days a week working in a pediatrician's office. The rest of her time is spent having fun with her family, working on her product line, scrapbooking, writing and volunteering at her church.

Please e-mail Allison at *scrapbookalley@aol.com*.
www.chickensoupforthescrapbookerssoul.com.

Who Is Debbie Haas?

Debbie was a stay-at-home mom for almost fifteen years, volunteering at church, school and within her community. As a foster mother, she loved many babies that came to her from drug-addicted mothers. After several years as a foster parent, she was able to adopt their youngest son to complete their family of four. Once the children were in school full-time, Debbie went back to work outside of the home.

Debbie started work at Colorbok as an executive administrative assistant to the vice-president of Memory in Craft. After only a few months, Debbie was promoted to the marketing events and education manager. Life as she knew it would never be the same. She began teaching scrapbooking classes at trade shows, consumer shows, cruise ships and numerous stores around the United States. It was more than a full-time job for her; it was a passion.

Now an independent consultant, Debbie has been a guest on the *Diva Craft Lounge World Talk Radio* show on several occasions. Debbie has been involved in product development and has been a designer for major manufacturers in the scrapbooking/paper crafting industry. She has been a marketing liaison and has been instrumental in bringing several companies together for the benefit of improving product development and packaging.

Debbie loves the ever-evolving world of scrapbooking and paper crafts. Helping people go to the next level, whether it is in one of her classes, at a trade show, in a "behind-the-scenes" meeting, designing samples or in product development, Debbie's enthusiasm is always contagious!

To contact Debbie Haas, e-mail her at *DebbieHaas@yahoo.com.*

Contributors

Several of the stories in this book were taken from previously published sources, such as books, magazines and newspapers. These sources are acknowledged in the permissions section. If you would like to contact any of the contributors for information about their writing or would like to invite them to speak in your community, look for their contact information included in their biographies.

The remainder of the stories were submitted by readers of our previous *Chicken Soup for the Soul* books who responded to our requests for stories. We have also included information about them.

Cathy Arnold, a scrapbook artist for over ten years, has been featured on *The Carol Duvall Show* and in *Creating Keepsakes* magazine. As editor of *Graceful Bee Online Scrapbook Magazine*, the first-ever Internet scrapbook magazine, she wrote *Memories to Capture*, along with hundreds of articles on every aspect of scrapbooking.

Mindy Barrow and her husband, Curtis, have been two peas in a pod since they met in 2001. Mindy enjoys scrapbooking, traveling, baking and listening to her husband recite his original poetry.

Hanni Baumgardner loves to play the piano, read or snuggle up with her shih tzu, Miyagi. She works as a freelance designer in a small town in Indiana.

Lisa Bearnson is the founder of *Creating Keepsakes* scrapbook magazine and the author of seven books. She hosts the monthly *Creative Keepsakes* hour on QVC and has appeared on several national television shows, including *Oprah* and the *Weekend Today Show*. She lives in Highland, Utah, with her husband and four children.

Paula F. Blevins lives in southern Ohio with her husband, three kids and many pets that keep multiplying. She enjoys working with kids and teaching Spanish. Paula is the author of the *For Hymn Mystery Series* and hopes to publish her children's books soon. Contact Paula through her Web site at *www.paulafblevins.com*.

Richard W. Bobbie holds a master's degree in Computer Science and has been working in the computer field for thirty years. He currently works on dispatch software for fire and ambulance services. He enjoys photography, Toastmasters, and wood and soapstone carving.

Amy R. Brown received her bachelor of arts, with honors, from the University of Idaho in 1998. She and her husband, Steve, have five children. With what's left of her time, she loves to scrapbook, read and take pictures. She also runs a photography business out of her home.

Betsy Burnett and her husband, Adam, live in Illinois with their children; Micaiah, Winter, David and Emily. When Betsy isn't busy with church or homeschooling activities, she enjoys writing, reading and scrapbooking. Betsy currently works with MemoryWorks as Creative Specialist and Faithfully Yours on their design team. Her email address is *lets_scrap@juno.com*.

Marnie L. Bushmole is currently a part of two promising design teams and is working on projects for various manufacturers and publications. She offers classes in quick paper crafting using stamps and various other mediums. Bringing this instant success to her students encourages them to continue delving into paper arts. Contact her at *Papertivity@aol.com*.

Patricia A. Cable received her BA in Linguistics in 1988. She married the following year and spent time as a technical writer and editor before becoming a stay-at-home mom to her two sons. Patricia enjoys scrapbooking, reading, writing and time with family.

Gwyn Calvetti is a professional storyteller who also happens to love travel, photography, scrapbooking and the great outdoors. When she's not telling stories or preparing dinner for her husband and two teenage sons, she's probably out birding. She lives in Wisconsin. Please e-mail her at *rcalvettijr@centurytel.net*.

Kathe Campbell lives on a 7,000-foot Montana mountain with her champion donkeys, her dog and a few kitties. Three grown children, eleven grands and three greats round out the herd. She has contributed to newspapers and national magazines on Alzheimer's disease. Her works include anthologies, magazines and medical journals. E-mail her at *bigskyadj@in-tch.com*.

Cynthia Chan resides in Maryland. She is married and the mother to five boys, including a set of triplets! She enjoys teaching scrapbooking to others at local stores and is well known for her cookie baking and hospitality. You can contact her at *blue_ribbon_design@yahoo.com*.

Jennifer Colannino is a lifelong resident of Rhode Island and currently teaches preschool in Cranston. She is an avid traveler who also enjoys photography, scrapbooking and spending time outdoors.

Lorie Couch is a working foster/adoptive mom who enjoys walking, reading, watching movies and scrapbooking.

Kelley Crisanti is a stay-at-home mom and wife. An avid reader, she started writing poetry as a child. Her scrapbooks are illustrations for her poems, memories and journaling. She finds inspiration in everyday life, especially her children Vince, Cathrynn and Olivia. Her hobbies include writing, scrapbooking and baking.

Merilyn J. Crittenden grew up in Brookfield, Illinois, and has been scrapbooking her life since childhood. She now lives in North Carolina with her husband, Ray. She has been a registered nurse since 1975, and also received her bachelor of arts in history from Old Dominion University in 1992. Please e-mail her at *mcritt@carolina.rr.com*.

Heather Dewaelsche has been a passionate scrapbooker for four years. She has had her layouts published in magazines and books, has won awards in several contests and is a designer for a scrapbook store. Heather lives in Indiana with her husband and their two children. Please e-mail her at *heatherdew@insightbb.com*.

Mack Dobbie received his BFA from the Center for Creative Studies in 1999. He works as a graphic designer and freelance illustrator. Besides drawing and painting Mack also enjoys playing guitar, learning foreign languages, and exploring the world of technology. You can contact him and view samples of his work at *mdobbie.com*.

Joel Doherty narrowly avoided a career in corporate aviation in favor of raising his four kids in the wilds of the great Northwest. He has written a fictional novel and is now working on a children's series entitled *Rebekah and the Magic Airplane*. Please e-mail him at *joel@northstatesinspections.com*.

Christina Dotson graduated from Ashland University in 2006 with a degree in Middle Childhood Education. Her articles and short stories, most written for children and teens, have appeared in numerous publications and anthologies. She plans to pursue a career as a middle-school teacher and author of books for young people. She may be reached at *chrissyd@accnorwalk.com*.

Deanna Doyle, a former teacher and librarian, is currently a scrapbook designer for various Web sites and manufacturers. The mother of two children and married for thirteen years, she resides in Pennsylvania. She is a former designer, writer and editor for *Scrapbooking.com* magazine and enjoys yoga, stamping, outdoor activities and reading.

Heather Ellis is a proud Air Force wife and stay-at-home mom. She holds a teaching degree from California State University Fullerton and loves helping out at her children's school. Heather shares her talents with Cub Scouts and enjoys scrapbooking with her mom and children.

Lisa Falduto worked in the field of Early Childhood Education for more than twenty years, helping children and families to identify and achieve goals. Currently, Lisa is involved in the scrapbooking world, designing pages for scrapbook manufacturers, custom pages for families, submitting designs for publication and teaching scrapbooking classes. E-mail her at *lfalduto@charter.net*.

Brenda Falk is a wife, mother of four and a homeschooling mom. She and her family reside in Michigan. She enjoys reading, crafts of various types, Bible study and friends.

Karen Flanigan is a dental hygienist in Tucson, Arizona. She is married to Chad, and they have two great kids, Katelyn and Riley. She enjoys traveling, photography and, of course, scrapbooking! She leads a scrapbooking group through her church. Please e-mail her at *thescrapbooker@comcast.net*.

Larae Mary Fowler was a teacher who became a stay-at-home mother for Rylin and Karyna. The Fowler family enjoys spending time together baking, gardening and playing at their Woodland, Connecticut, home.

Katherine Freeman and her husband recently moved to Florida to enjoy a more relaxed lifestyle. While working at the local children's hospital, she spends her spare time with her three major loves—her family, the ocean, and scrapbooking. Her circle of incredible friends has grown and prospered through this wonderful hobby.

Jennifer S. Gallacher began working in the scrapbook industry in 1997 for *PaperKuts Magazine*. Since that time she has worked as a freelance designer for Making Memories, Li'l Davis Designs, Karen Foster Design and Deja Views. Her designs have been showcased in more than one hundred publications. You may contact her at *js_gallacher@hotmail.com*.

Leeza Gibbons has been called a social entrepreneur, but if you ask Leeza Gibbons what she does, she'll simply answer, "I'm a storyteller." From television news journalist to radio personality, producer and businesswoman, Leeza has been entering America's living rooms for more than twenty-five years.

Paula Gunter-Best received her bachelor of arts with high honors from Eckerd College, St. Petersburg, Florida, in 1997. Her love for children, animals and scrapbooking provide the resources for an emerging independent ministry utilizing her talents and interests. She can be reached at *best.paula@gmail.com*.

Jlyne Hanback is a freelance scrapbook artist and enjoys many different types of paper crafting. She has been published in virtually every major scrapbooking publication and has designed for *Chatterbox* for the last three years. She truly loves working with other people, teaching scrapbooking/paper arts classes in her spare time.

Karen Helsen received her bachelor's degree in business from Aquinas College and her master of science degree in Information Systems Management from Ferris State University. She is self-employed in the ornamental nursery industry in Western Michigan. Karen enjoys raising her three children with her husband and best friend, Greg. She also enjoys scrapbooking, the great outdoors, hiking, playing volleyball and reading.

Sarah Higgins received her bachelor of music in Music Education from Brenau University in 1997 and her Master of Education from North Georgia College and State University in 2000. She taught for seven years. Sarah enjoys scrapbooking, reading, music and spending time with her family.

Jennifer Howland is a former television and newspaper reporter from North

Adams, Massachusetts. She currently works at home and is raising three beautiful children with her husband Jason. She loves scrapbooking, writing, and photography. She has also returned to college to pursue a nursing degree. You can contact Jennifer at *khowlets@yahoo.com*.

Suzanne Kigler lives in Virginia and is the mother of two handsome boys. Suzanne started scrapbooking five years ago with her sisters. Since then, Suzanne has scrapbooked many memories and stories about her life and experiences. It is because of scrapbooking that Suzanne was able to connect with the love of her life once again.

Stacey Kingman received her bachelor of arts from Texas A & M University in 1990. Her creations have been featured in various scrapbooking and paper crafting publications. She teaches her four children at home, her favorite color is lime green, and she can be found scrapping at night while her family sleeps.

Sharon Knopic became a scrapbooker upon the sudden death of her mother over a decade ago. Since then she has taught at various conventions nationwide and considers journaling more important than the photos. She enjoys spending time with her grown son and many pets outside of Hershey, Pennsylvania.

Maggie Koller received her BS in psychology and her teaching certification from Eastern Michigan University in 1997 and 2005, respectively. She is a high-school English teacher and avid scrapbook instructor in Michigan. She also serves as the newsletter editor for a national scrapbooking company. Please e-mail her at *scrappymags@yahoo.com*.

Jennifer Kranenburg is a single mother to three young children and also a full-time student in the Early Childhood Education program, with hopes of continuing on to the university and becoming a teacher. Jennifer enjoys scrapbooking, volunteering in the community, photography, teaching scrapbook classes and has organized a charity crop.

Jessica LaGrossa received her bachelor of communications with honors from Reinhardt College (Waleska, Georgia) in 2001. She is an associate editor for *Advance Newsmagazine* in King of Prussia, Pennsylvania. Jessi, as her friends call her, is an avid reader and tackles any craft project involving patterned paper! A Southern gal at heart, Jessi is learning to enjoy the cold northeast with her devoted husband, Chris, and their loyal dog, Josie.

Adrienne Lehtinen received her BA from McGill University in 1993. She is a stay-at-home mom to two exceptional children who are bravely surmounting health challenges. She loves good jokes and appreciates the friends and family who overlook the really bad ones. Adrienne also enjoys traveling, especially to her husband's homeland of Finland.

Nancy Ann Liedel enjoys a zany life. Married for twelve years, she is the mother of two adopted boys, Eugene and Steven, and two birth children, "Surprise and Shock" (really, Herne and Gerald). Travel and slow triathlons are

Nancy's passions. Her goals include completing an Ironman. Please send e-mail to *Nancy@liedel.org*.

Tamara Limestahl is a married, stay-at-home mother of five: four boys and a girl. She enjoys scrapbooking, reading, writing, watching the Food and Style networks, and taking care of her family. She is currently working on a fiction novel.

Mary Mason now makes her home in Dallas, Texas, with her husband, Mike, fourteen-year-old stepson, John, three crazy cats and one beta fish. She is an audit trainer and writes technical materials for her job, and she loves scrapbooking, quilting, gardening, music and theater. Please e-mail her at *mmason51@comcast.net*.

Ginger McSwain is a paralegal turned storybook and scrapbook artist who lives in Cary, North Carolina. Ginger loves combining her love of photography with varied journaling styles to suit the story she is trying to tell. Please e-mail her at *gmcswain@nc.rr.com*.

Stephanie Menzock is the executive director to her husband, Chuck, and daughters, Autumn and Brooke. Stephanie has had a love for writing since she was a teenager. Her work is published in *The National Library of Poetry, Question of Balance*.

Nikki Merson is a photographer and scrapbooker in St. Louis, Missouri. She is married to Jeff, stepmom to Ashlon, and mom to Riley, America, Alana and Amelia. Her first artistic passion is photography; scrapbooking is her way of forever capturing the blessings in her life. Please e-mail her at *nikkimerson@directway.com*.

Ami Mizell-Flint is married to John and has three children, Megan, Matthew and Jacob. She lives in San Angelo, Texas, where she co-owns Scrapbook University with Jody Waters. She enjoys playing with her kids, traveling, cooking and, of course, scrapbooking.

Arielle Napp graduated from Danbury High School, Connecticut, in 2005. She is currently a freshman studying anthropology at the University of Delaware. She sends love to Daddy, Alex, Lovebug, RP11 and the Flos at UD. She says, "Mommy, thank you for celebrating every moment of my life. I love you!" E-mail her at *anapp@udel.edu*.

Patricia Nelson is first and foremost a mother and daughter. She has been an author as well as a teacher in the scrapbook industry since 1998. She prides herself on being a modern scrapbook artist and throughly enjoys her craft with enthusiasm. She also enjoys photography and traveling with her family.

Cheryl Neumann teaches scrapbooking classes for children in northeastern North Dakota. Cheryl loves sharing new techniques with her students, family and friends. Cheryl and her husband, Mike, have six children and one grandson. She has been scrapbooking for her family for twenty years. Cheryl has been a special education teacher for twenty-nine years and has loved every moment!

Mark Parisi's "Off the Mark" comic panel has been syndicated since 1987 and is distributed by United Media. Mark's humor also graces greeting cards, T-shirts, calendars, magazines, newsletters and books. Please visit his Web site at: *www.offthemark.com*. Lynn is his wife/business partner and their daughter, Jenny, contributes with inspiration, (as do three cats).

Angie Pedersen is the author of the best-selling *Book of Me* series of books on scrapbook journaling. She is also the editor of two award-winning Web sites, *www.onescrappysite.com* and *www.scrapyourstories.com*. She lives in Kansas City, Missouri, with her husband and two children. She welcomes your feedback at *angie@onescrappysite.com*.

Holly Pittroff is a stay-at-home-mom and professional scrapbooker in North Carolina. She is a designer for Keller's Creations (*www.acidfree.com*), a scrapbooking product company owned by Kim Mock. Holly's work has been published in a variety of scrapbooking and craft magazines, and her goal is to design full-time for one of the larger scrapbooking publications.

Carol McAdoo Rehme collects people, paper, paraphernalia and precious memories—all the ingredients necessary for scrapbooking. Carol is a longtime author and editor for the *Chicken Soup for the Soul* series. The newly released *Chicken Soup for the Soul Christmas Virtues* is her first book. Contact her at *carol@rehme.com* or *www.rehme.com*.

Donna Rogers wrote *The Menopause Survival Guide*, edits *Midlife Monthly* e-Newsletter, contributes to *My Time Alone* devotionals and mentors Christian women online. She hosted a radio ministry with her husband and has been a guest on TV and radio. Donna enjoys family, friends, writing and e-mails. Contact her at *www.DonnaRogers.com*.

Lisa M. Sanford has been "addicted" to scrapbooking for the past nine years. She's planning a book about her style of scrapbooking, *Ethnic Scrapbooking: Infusing Your Scrapbooks with Cultural Flair.*

Alonnya Schemer has been writing since the age of nine, everything from novels to songs. She has always enjoyed it. God told her when she was nine that she was to use this talent for his glory, and that is an awesome opportunity. Her greatest inspiration for the stories that she writes comes from the people she loves most and, most especially, her beloved nephews—children who see the world through such innocent eyes, who love wholeheartedly and unreservedly, as God intends all his children to. Please e-mail her at *aschemer@aol.com*.

Andy Skidmore has had stories in several *Chicken Soup for the Soul* books. She loves to write and photograph scenes and/or objects that relate to her stories. She is the wife of one, mother of two and grandmother of three. She is writing a book for each grandchild and gives them as Christmas presents, one page of their book each year. Contact her at *AndySkid@aol.com*.

Rhonda W. Sneeden received her BS and MA from East Carolina University. She has taught exceptional children for more than twenty-nine years. She is married and has two sons. She loves scrapbooking, reading and traveling. Her dream is to be published in a *Chicken Soup* book. Please e-mail her at *sky8284@yahoo.com*.

Cindy Lee Sparks lives in Nebraska with her husband, Bruce, and their five cats. As an amateur writer, this will be the first time she has had a story published. She would love to write a book in the future, sharing her faith, as well as her love of scrapbooking.

Colleen Stearns teaches middle-school English in Pennsylvania. She is a member of the Junkitz and Scrapping with Style design teams and does freelance artwork for *Memory Makers Magazine*. Colleen enjoys scrapbooking, writing and spending time with her husband, Jim, and two sons, Jacob and Ian. E-mail her at *colleenstearns@hotmail.com*.

Christine Stoneman received her bachelor of science in 1991 and her master's of science in 1996. She works as a biologist for the Canadian federal government. Christine enjoys traveling, photography, wilderness canoeing and, of course, scrapbooking. She lives with her husband, Mike, in Ottawa, Canada.

Melissa Tharp resides in Maryland with her husband and two cats. She enjoys scrapbooking, playing the piano, singing, reading and writing. Although never published, she has written over fifty songs and twenty five poems. Melissa's dream is to become a writer of Christian novels one day.

Joan Thezan is a native of northwest Missouri. She works as a high-school secretary and cheerleading coach. In addition to scrapbooking, Joan's hobbies include reading and counted cross-stitch. She continually works to improve her photography skills. Please contact Joan at *bjthezan@earthlink.net*.

Lisa Ray Turner graduated from the University of Michigan with a master's in music, then began writing and raising three sons. She's the author of five books, teaches humanities and writing, and works as an editor. Lisa lives with her husband and three sons. E-mail her at *PinkDiva@aol.com*.

Stacey Wakelin is a stay-at-home mom; children Evan and Taylor, are constant sources of inspiration. Since starting scrapbooking in 2001, Stacey has been published in several scrapbooking publications. One highlight is teaching at Clipper Street Scrapbook Co. in Langley, BC. Stacey can be reached at *swakelin @telus.net*.

Suzanne Walker is an enthusiastic crafter and mother of three who enjoys scrapbooking and heirloom sewing, as well as painting and creative home décor. She has led numerous scrapbooking seminars and events for every age group—from Scout troops to nursing homes and currently hosts a crafting web show for Fiskars.

Eugene Arthur Woods is retired with his wife. He enjoys painting pictures on canvas, gardening, spending time with family and his grandchildren. When he has time, he scrapbooks for his children and grandchildren.

Perfect inspiration

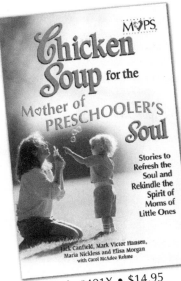

Code #401X • $14.95

Code #4036 • $14.95

Code #088X • $14.95

Also Available

Chicken Soup African American Soul
Chicken Soup Body and Soul
Chicken Soup Bride's Soul
Chicken Soup Caregiver's Soul
Chicken Soup Cat Lover's Soul
Chicken Soup Christian Family Soul
Chicken Soup Christian Soul
Chicken Soup College Soul
Chicken Soup Couple's Soul
Chicken Soup Dog Lover's Soul
Chicken Soup Dieter's Soul
Chicken Soup Expectant Mother's Soul
Chicken Soup Father's Soul
Chicken Soup Fisherman's Soul
Chicken Soup Girlfriend's Soul
Chicken Soup Golden Soul
Chicken Soup Golfer's Soul, Vol. I, II
Chicken Soup Horse Lover's Soul, Vol. I, II
Chicken Soup Inspire a Woman's Soul
Chicken Soup Kid's Soul, Vol. I, II
Chicken Soup Mother's Soul, Vol. I, II
Chicken Soup Nature Lover's Soul
Chicken Soup Parent's Soul
Chicken Soup Pet Lover's Soul
Chicken Soup Preteen Soul, Vol. I, II
Chicken Soup Single's Soul
Chicken Soup Shopper's Soul
Chicken Soup Soul, Vol. I-VI
Chicken Soup at Work
Chicken Soup Sports Fan's Soul
Chicken Soup Teenage Soul, Vol. I-IV
Chicken Soup Woman's Soul, Vol. I, II

Available wherever books are sold.
To order direct: Telephone (800) 441-5569 • www.hcibooks.com
Prices do not include shipping and handling. Your response code is CCS.